T0281810

Mobile Disruptions in the Middle East

Mobile Disruptions in the Middle East identifies trends in mobile media use in Qatar and the United Arab Emirates and, more broadly, explores their impact on the nature of digital journalism. Mobility has long been an important aspect of life in the Middle East; therefore a study of this region presents a unique opportunity to examine the role of mobile media and its future directions.

Basing its analysis on original research, including multiyear surveys and case studies, the book reveals patterns of audience engagement with mobile media in the Gulf area, with particular emphasis on online journalism. The research also illustrates how and to what extent media organizations are developing and delivering content uniquely designed for mobile media and consumption. Drawing on these findings, the authors look at possible developments in mobile media content strategies, including those for news content, as wearable and other emerging media forms enter the marketplace.

Mobile Disruptions in the Middle East provides an important insight into a region that is both globally active and mobile-first, yet whose use of digital media is historically under-researched. As a result, the book helps to advance understanding of consumer preference for content types on mobile media, especially in relation to the transformation of journalism.

John V. Pavlik is Professor in the Department of Journalism and Media Studies at the School of Communication and Information, Rutgers, the State University of New Jersey, USA.

Everette E. Dennis is Dean and CEO of Northwestern University in Qatar and Professor in Northwestern's Medill School, USA.

Rachel Davis Mersey is Associate Professor at the Medill School of Journalism, Media, Integrated Marketing Communications and Faculty Fellow at the Institute for Policy Research at Northwestern University, USA.

Justin Gengler is Assistant Research Professor at the Social and Economic Survey Research Institute (SESRI) at Qatar University.

Disruptions: Studies in Digital Journalism
Series editor: Bob Franklin

Disruptions refers to the radical changes provoked by the affordances of digital technologies that occur at a pace and on a scale that disrupts settled understandings and traditional ways of creating value, interacting and communicating both socially and professionally. The consequences for digital journalism involve far reaching changes to business models, professional practices, roles, ethics, products and even challenges to the accepted definitions and understandings of journalism. For Digital Journalism Studies, the field of academic inquiry which explores and examines digital journalism, disruption results in paradigmatic and tectonic shifts in scholarly concerns. It prompts reconsideration of research methods, theoretical analyses and responses (oppositional and consensual) to such changes, which have been described as being akin to 'a moment of mind blowing uncertainty'.

Routledge's new book series, *Disruptions: Studies in Digital Journalism*, seeks to capture, examine and analyse these moments of exciting and explosive professional and scholarly innovation which characterize developments in the day-to-day practice of journalism in an age of digital media, and which are articulated in the newly emerging academic discipline of Digital Journalism Studies.

Responsible Drone Journalism
Astrid Gynnild and Turo Uskali

Mobile Disruptions in the Middle East
Lessons from Qatar and the Arabian Gulf Region in mobile media content innovation
John V. Pavlik, Everette E. Dennis, Rachel Davis Mersey, and Justin Gengler

For a full list of titles in this series, please visit the Routledge website: www.routledge.com/Disruptions/book-series/DISRUPTDIGJOUR

Mobile Disruptions in the Middle East

Lessons from Qatar and the
Arabian Gulf region in mobile
media content innovation

**John V. Pavlik, Everette E. Dennis,
Rachel Davis Mersey, and
Justin Gengler**

Routledge
Taylor & Francis Group

LONDON AND NEW YORK

First published 2018 by Routledge

2 Park Square, Milton Park, Abingdon, Oxon OX14 4RN
605 Third Avenue, New York, NY 10017

Routledge is an imprint of the Taylor & Francis Group, an informa business

First issud in paperback 2021

Library of Congress Cataloging-in-Publication Data
A catalog record for this book has been requested

ISBN: 978-1-138-05005-1 (hbk)
ISBN: 978-1-03-217873-8 (pbk)
DOI: 10.4324/9781315169118

Typeset in Times New Roman
by Apex CoVantage, LLC

We offer special thanks to the Qatar National Research Fund for providing the grant to support the data we have reported in this book.

Contents

List of figures   viii
List of tables   ix

1   Mobility, media and Qatar   1

2   Innovation and media disruption   10

3   Mobile media   23

4   Mobile media in Qatar and the Gulf   35

5   Public engagement   61

6   Media adaptation in the Gulf   82

7   Concluding reflections: trends in the next generation
    of journalism and media   94

    Index   99

Figures

2.1	The evolution of disruption theory	14
2.2	The four domains of media	18
2.3	U.S. 5G rollout timeline	20
3.1	Adopters of innovations	25
3.2	Strategies for digital content innovation	27
3.3	Content innovation strategies for mobile, digital media	28
3.4	Type IV content: mobile and user-optimized	29
4.1	Three-year investigation of mobile media content innovation	38
5.1	Interest in mobile media content type by subject salience in Qatar	70
5.2	Interest in mobile media content type by subject salience in the UAE	71
5.3	Interest in mobile media content type by education level in Qatar, controlling for subject salience	73
5.4	Interest in mobile media content type by education level in the UAE, controlling for subject salience	74
5.5	Interest in mobile media content type by age in Qatar, controlling for subject salience	75
5.6	Interest in mobile media content type by age in Qatar, controlling for subject salience	76
5.7	Interest in mobile media content type of Qataris only by age (dichotomous), controlling for subject salience	76
5.8	Interest in mobile media content type of Qataris only by age (5 categories), controlling for subject salience	77
5.9	Interest in mobile media content type of Emiratis only by age (dichotomous), controlling for subject salience	77
5.10	Interest in mobile media content type of Emiratis only by age (5 categories), controlling for subject salience	78

Tables

4.1   Sample size frequency (N) in Qatar, Year 1, 2016   43
4.2   Sample size frequency (N) in Qatar, Year 2, 2017   43
4.3   Q15a. Interest in augmented reality (AR) in Qatar, Year 1   49
4.4   Q15b. Interest in augmented reality (AR) in Qatar, Year 2   49
4.5   Tabular data: Q19a. Interest in virtual reality (VR) in
      Qatar, Year 1   50
4.6   Tabular data: Q19b. Interest in virtual reality (VR) in
      Qatar, Year 2   50

1   Mobility, media and Qatar

Introduction

Mobility has long been an important aspect of life in the Middle East and in the Arab Gulf in particular. Therefore the region presents a unique opportunity to examine the role of mobile media, which we do in Qatar and the United Arab Emirates (UAE) specifically and explore deeply in this book.

The main themes and objectives are threefold. First, we examine audience engagement with mobile media, including broad areas such as Internet use to more specific content such as journalism. Doing such work in an area that has been historically underresearched by comparison to the West, we are able to provide insight on a region that is both globally active and mobile-first. Penetration of smartphones in Qatar and the UAE, for example, outpace rates in the United States. In addition, Qatar, the UAE and the rest of the Gulf states are vitally important places of study in regard to mobile media use because the region's tradition of communication and mobility frame the contemporary age of mobile media.

Second, complementary to our analysis of audience engagement with mobile media content, including news, is a focus on how media organizations adapt to and respond to mobile media – in particular, how and to what extent media are operating in Qatar and the Gulf in developing and delivering content uniquely designed for mobile media and consumption.

Third, from the basis of our study, we explore possible future directions in mobile media content strategies, including news, as wearable and other emerging media forms enter the marketplace. While the media industry has begun to experiment with content for emerging technologies, we recognize the need for evidence-based reasoning for further content development.

This book offers a perspective on the development of content for mobile media. We draw on original research evidence collected in Qatar and the Gulf region. The data this book is based on are part of a three-year study funded by the Qatar National Research Fund (Pavlik, Dennis, Mersey and Gengler, 2013). This project represents one of the first systematic large-scale studies of mobile media innovation, especially in the context of content design. As such, it helps to advance understanding of consumer preference for content types on mobile media, especially the transformation of journalism in the region.

This is a data-driven examination of mobile media innovation, in Qatar and the UAE, two advanced-technology sophisticated societies. This innovation is leading to a transformation of the media landscape in the region, giving rise to more public engagement and interaction. We also offer evidence about production and consumption patterns. This yields a set of "best practices" in the development of mobile media content in the region.

Just-released data on global Internet penetration underscores the appropriateness of focusing this examination on Qatar and the United Arab Emirates at this time. In particular, the 2018 Global Digital suite of reports published on 31 January 2018 reveal that Qatar and the UAE have the highest Internet penetration in the world. Internet penetration in each country is 99%. Moreover, not only has global Internet penetration continued to grow to its highest levels (4 billion of the world's 7.6 billion persons, or 53%), but so has mobile device usage. As 2018 Global Digital reports, "More than 200 million people got their first mobile device in 2017, and two-thirds of the world's 7.6 billion inhabitants now have a mobile phone" (Global Digital, 2018).

Cultural and historical context of mobility

As noted, mobility has a strong and deep cultural and sociological foundation in Qatar and the Arabian Gulf region with the movement of Bedouin tribes and their traditions shaping the lifestyle and values of the Gulf (Ferdinand, 1993). This connected well with the development of trading routes and settlements where individual communication played an essential role.

Moreover, a heritage of interpersonal communication played a significant role in the region (Mitchell and Marriage, 2006). Whether in the form of the *majlis*, a traditional gathering place, in a vital communication channel, or in a mosque, interpersonal communication has featured prominently in Islamic societies. Thus it was not incongruous when the National Broadband Plan for the State of Qatar was released in December 2013 to document the strategic importance of mobile broadband technology in the future of Qatar (National Broadband Plan, 2013).

What the literature tells us

Scholars note that mobility is an important matter in the Middle East, including in Qatar. But they add, "Mobility in the Middle East is a challenging prospect" (Esfahani, 2016). For one, mobility has evolved greatly in the Middle East in the past century. "Long before mechanized vehicles became the norm, people solely relied on walking or animal transport. Hence, domesticated camels have always been an intrinsic part of the Middle Eastern landscape." The deserts and shifting sand dunes are a geographic dimension that affects mobility in Qatar and throughout the Middle East. Especially strong winds, sometimes called the *qibli* in Arabic and the *sirocco* in Europe, sometimes reach hurricane force and can make building and maintaining roads a challenge.

The aridity of the desert also presents a great challenge to mobility in Qatar, the Gulf and in the Middle East region. Waterways, including the Gulf, have long played an important role in mobility in Qatar and the Gulf region. Wind-propelled sailboats, such as the dhow, were a principal means of transportation and trade.

In modern times, both land-based automobiles and water-based taxis have helped close the gap between time and distance in the Gulf. Following on development in Dubai, Qatar is in the midst of the development of even more advanced systems for public mass transit, including rail, light rail and a subway. Moreover, Doha has emerged as a major hub not only for the region but for the world, via both an ultramodern airport and seaport.

Mobility in Qatar and the Gulf region is also shaped by cultural and politi- cal contexts. In Fromherz's (2013) history of Qatar, the historian recalls the words of one of the country's historical leaders. "'We are all from the highest to the lowest slaves of one master, [the] Pearl" (p. 114), the sole source of trade and commerce at the time. "In this way a local chieftain, Muhammad Ibn Thani, summarised the Qatari condition for the benefit of the English traveller William Palgrave." As Fromherz explains, Ibn Thani offered this observation in 1863. At the time, the British Empire had devel- oped interest in the remote peninsula in part for reasons of transport and global commerce. In less than a decade, "Colonel Pelly, having invited all the local sheikhs aboard the ship *Vigilant*, was to name that same Muham- mad Ibn Thani as the only interlocutor of the English government. Modern Qatar was born."

Through the 1920s, Qatar's economy depended on pearl fishing, and the country was home to some 60,000 pearl fishers. In 1971, Qatar gained its independence from British rule and is today a monarchy ruled by an emir from the royal Al Thani dynasty. By 2017, Qatar had a population of 300,000 nationals and another 2.2 million expatriates, bringing Qatar's total population to 2.5 million (Al Araby, 2016). Qatar's economy has grown rap- idly, largely derived from rich fields of natural gas. Consequently, as writes Gray (2013), "Qatar has risen rapidly from obscurity to become the world's wealthiest country per capita."

Fromherz notes that while Qatar has seen tremendous economic change and associated advances in infrastructure, its political and social systems have been relatively stable. "So much has changed in the infrastructure and physical, built environment of Qatar. So little has changed within the Qatari citizen's basic social milieu" (p. 13).

Qatar has emerged as an independent state and a monarchy. Notably, Qatar has virtually no potable water, and as such is dependent on foreign trade, as well as its desalination plants, for this vital resource (Kamrava, 2013).

Vital to the country's modern condition has been the development of the television and online journalism and media network Al Jazeera. Fromherz explains that it provided extensive news coverage of the Arab revolutions especially in Egypt, Libya and Syria. As such, Ulrichsen (2014) notes that it has contributed to growing pressure on Qatar from Saudi Arabia and the United Arab Emirates to reverse the country's support for the Muslim Brotherhood. The first successful such satellite network in the region, it has established a footprint across the region and has inspired competitors and jealousy.

The predominant presence of expatriates has enabled Qataris to enjoy the fruits of modernity. Fromherz adds, "The price. . . is the existence of an expatriate culture. However, this expatriate culture is kept subservient, in terms of rights and access to Qatar's economy" (p. 10).

Modernity has also brought significant levels of mobile communications and high-speed Internet access. These have been vital to both the expat communities and the modern economy, as well as to Qataris.

Media observers have long been intrigued by and have offered perspectives on the Middle East. Many of these perspectives often have been deeply flawed by inaccuracies and portrayals characterized by misunderstandings of Islam and Islamic culture. This has been true of the Middle East in general and of Qatar in particular.

This problem in media representation was exacerbated in 2017 as a diplomatic conflict between Qatar and several of its Gulf neighbors, including the Kingdom of Saudi Arabia (KSA) and the UAE, emerged, and Western media have faced a great challenge in reporting the multifaceted story thoroughly and with nuance and context. It has been especially vexing to Western news media as part of a list of demands for change that the KSA-led group submitted to Qatar was the complete closure of Al Jazeera, which has sometimes proved critical of some of the Gulf states and is also a source of relative journalism independence and press freedom in a region long somewhat bereft in this regard.

In Chapter 6, we further discuss the blockade of Qatar in greater detail, but it is replete with a cautionary tale for mobile and social media. While digital communication and mobility have helped Qatar, the Gulf and the larger Middle East leapfrog other technologies – cable, satellite radio and others – it has also been the source of grave threats to security. A hacked website in Qatar, later documented to be the mischief of operatives in the UAE, as well as the spreading of false news and other distortions, provided a rationale for the siege of Qatar that had entered its eighth month as this book was being written. With threats of armed conflict and a vigorous information war among the parties, the blockade became a geopolitical hot spot and drew in major powers, while ending any semblance of solidarity among the Gulf nations, represented in the Gulf Cooperation Council (GCC). Amid the charges and countercharges among the blockading countries and Qatar came a tweet from U.S. President Donald Trump siding with the Saudis and their allies that contradicted statements by his own secretaries of state and defense. From a simple hack and its aftermath came an avalanche of international and Middle East media coverage spurred by massive public relations efforts. The result was many hardships and displacements, ranging from travel issues, to food supply, family disruption and the constant threat of possible armed conflict. In this instance, mobile communication was not only a conduit but a main stage player as well.

At about the time Qatar was emerging onto the world's stage as a significant economic force, Edward Said published his classic work *Orientalism* (1978). Said's critical examination articulated how Western media have often demonized Islam and its followers. Said adds historical context to his analysis, noting the role of mobility in understanding the Middle East, or the "Orient." "Bracketed between the enduring hostilities of the Renaissance and the rigid academic taxonomies of the nineteenth century, the eighteenth century thus appears unique as a time of flexibility, mobility, and possibility as regards European relationships with and representations of the Orient" (p. 7).

The rise and confluence of social media and mobile media bring important implications to Qatar and the Gulf region. Gunter, Elareshi and Al-Jaber (2016) note that, following the Arab Spring, social media use became instrumental in organizing activist movements and spreading political dissent in the Middle East. The consequences are far-reaching and potentially disruptive, they explain. There are implications for the status of women in Kuwait, for example, as well as for the political, social and religious identities of citizens.

A notable confluence of mobile media, social media and social norms occurred in KSA in July of 2017. Video surfaced of a woman walking through a KSA historical site, which had been shot via a mobile device and posted online to the woman's social media network site. Its publication and airing on television news caused an uproar in KSA and the Gulf region, as women are banned from going out in public in KSA without being completely covered. The woman was subsequently arrested, although she was ultimately released. Social media responses to the situation ranged widely across the social and political spectrum, with some supporting her acts (which would not likely have raised so much as an eyebrow in the West) as a feminist right and others condemning her (Domonoske, 2017).

Historical perspective on mobility in media

Globally, mobility long has influenced journalism and media. Examples of mobile media innovations are abundant, such as Reuters 19th-century experiments with carrier pigeons to deliver the news (Reuters, 2008). In fact, the invention of the printing press set the stage for media mobility. The advent of printing enabled the large-scale production of mobile media forms including the book and the newspaper. Nineteenth-century advances in printing technology enabled the mass production of books and newspapers that readers could easily carry with them. The initial development of electronic communication in the form of the wireless, or radio, and later television necessitated audiences to purchase listening and viewing devices, or sets, that were used in fixed locations. But this situation gradually changed, especially due to the invention of the transistor in the 1950s. This gave rise to portable, handheld radio receivers and later converged with the computer to produce digital media devices. With the invention of the Internet, the 21st century has witnessed a digital and mobile media development on a scale comparable to Gutenberg's printing press. Just as the printing press led to widespread social and cultural transformation including the Renaissance, the mobile, digital and connected media of the 21st century are fueling far-reaching change and disruption. Further fueling the disruption are the emergence of mobile telecommunications and its convergence in digital devices with mediated and Internet access. This means that today citizens and expatriates alike in Qatar and elsewhere have access to interactive mobile communications devices that give them continuous and instant access to news, information, entertainment and interpersonal communication that can span the globe at a very low, affordable cost.

These mobile media and communications enable not only journalism and other legacy media to distribute content to the public. They also enable users or members of the public to engage in or participate in an interactive communication process.

This convergence of mobile media and communications therefore makes Qatar and the UAE an ideal setting for the groundbreaking research reported in this book.

Mobile media are rapidly diffusing around the world, and a growing body of research is examining mobile media use, especially among different demographic groups. Katz (2008) has examined the unique qualities of mobile media use. Among the findings are differences in mobile media use in private versus public settings and the rise of selfies (photos taken by the photographer of her- or himself) as a photographic form of visual communication in a mobile media environment (Katz and Crocker, 2015a, 2015b).

A growing amount of research evidence indicates that the audience for journalism is increasingly moving toward mobile-only consumption. A 2017 report from the UK suggests that the majority of news consumers in that country now rely exclusively on their mobile device to access and engage the news, at least for the news produced and delivered by the six largest newspapers in that country. Specifically, a National Readership Survey (NRS) shows that more than 70% of the audience for the largest six newspapers in the UK are mobile-only users (Ciobanu, 2017). Some are well over 70%. In particular:

> *The Independent*, which stopped publishing its print edition a little over one year ago, has the largest share of mobile-only national audience, at 85.3 per cent, followed by the *Daily Mirror* (79.3 per cent), *The Telegraph* (75.6 per cent), *the Guardian* (75.5 per cent), *The Sun* (74.6 per cent) and *the Daily Mail* (72.2 per cent).

Similar trends are seen in the United States and are expected to grow in the next five years. Two-thirds of news consumption will likely be via mobile in the United States by 2020, and mobile news consumption is growing fastest among minority segments of the U.S. population, including Latinos, Blacks and low-income Americans (Dunaway, 2016). The implications for Qatar are especially apparent in the context of that country's hosting of the 2022 FIFA soccer (football) world championship, when potentially more than a million fans may descend on the country from Europe and elsewhere, bringing with them their expectations of engaging in a heavy and interactive diet of soccer (football) news via their mobile devices.

Beyond such studies, relatively little research has examined the development of content uniquely designed for the mobile platform. Moreover, little of the existing research looks specifically at the Middle East, especially Qatar and the Gulf region, as well as the potential transformative influences of mobile media content innovation and usage.

Weber and Hussain (2018) have examined the expanding use of social media in the Middle East, including Qatar. They have also examined related communication developments, including growing health awareness in the region as reflected in social media communication, the reflection of national identity in social media, and the nature of social media communication in multilingual cultures such as Qatar.

This book addresses the unique role that content plays in the rise of mobile communication in Qatar and the Gulf region. Evidence presented here is based on preliminary findings from a three-year research investigation funded by a grant provided by the Qatar National Research Fund. Findings are provided from a multiyear and multicountry survey, detailed media industry case studies, and a quasi-experimental examination of public engagement with mobile media content. Analysis at both the theoretical and practical levels will examine the extent to which mobile media content engages the public in Qatar and the Gulf and what content strategies media organizations are developing for the mobile platform. Innovation is a key factor, but its form and function are still evolving for the mobile and increasingly wearable environment. We will consider implications for future mobile media applications in Qatar, in the Gulf and around the world, especially as mobile media become increasingly ubiquitous and as next-generation media, such as wearable devices, enter the marketplace.

References

Al Araby. (2 March 2016). "Migrant Workers Propel Qatar's Population to 2.5 Million." Retrieved 7 August 2017 from www.alaraby.co.uk/english/amp/news/2016/3/2/migrant-workers-propel-qatars-population-to-2-5-million

Ciobanu, Mădălina. (26 June 2017). "NRS: More Than 70 Percent of the National Audience of 6 UK Papers Is Mobile-Only." Retrieved 1 July 2017 from www.journalism.co.uk/news/nrs-more-than-70-per-cent-of-the-national-audience-of-6-uk-papers-is-mobile-only/s2/a706272/

Domonoske, Camila. (18 July 2017). "Woman in Saudi Arabia Arrested for Wearing Skirt, Crop Top in Video." Retrieved 7 August 2017 from www.npr.org/sections/thetwo-way/2017/07/18/537925382/woman-in-saudi-arabia-arrested-for-wearing-skirt-crop-top-in-video

Dunaway, Johanna. (30 August 2016). "Mobile vs. Computer: Implications for News Audiences and Outlets." Joan Shorenstein Center, Harvard University. Retrieved 1 July 2017 from http://shorensteincenter.org/mobile-vs-computer-news-audiences-and-outlets/

Esfahani, Hadi Saleh. (2016). "Mobility in the Middle East." Center for South Asian and Middle Eastern Studies, University of Illinois at Urbana–Champaign. Retrieved 25 May 2017 from www.csames.illinois.edu/documents/outreach/Mobility-Middle_East.pdf

Ferdinand, Klaus. (1993). *The Bedouins of Qatar.* Retrieved 5 January 2018 from www.everyculture.com/No-Sa/Qatar.html#ixzz2jZ2gp7D4

Fromherz, Allen J. (2013). *Qatar: A Modern History*. London: I. B. Tauris. Global Digital. (2018). "Digital in 2018." Retrieved 7 February 2018 from https://wearesocial.com/blog/2018/01/global-digital-report-2018

Gray, Matthew. (2013). *Qatar and the Politics of Development*. Boulder, CO: Lynne Rienner.

Gunter, Barrie, Mokhtar Elareshi and Khalid Al-Jaber, eds. (2016). *Social Media in the Arab World: Communication and Public Opinion in the Gulf States*. London: I. B. Tauris & Co.

Kamrava, Mehran. (2013). *Qatar: Small State, Big Politics*. Utica, NY: Cornell University Press.

Katz, James E., ed. (2008). *Handbook of Mobile Communication Studies*. Cambridge, MA: MIT Press.

Katz, James E. and Elizabeth Thomas Crocker. (2015a). "Skype in Daily Life: General Patterns, Emerging Uses, and Concerns." In José Ricardo Carvalheiro and Ana Serrano Tellería (eds.), *Mobile and Digital Communication: Approaches to Public and Private*. Covilhã, Portugal: LabCom Books, University of Beira Interior, pp. 5–23.

Katz, James E. and Elizabeth Thomas Crocker. (2015b). "Selfies and Photo Messaging as Visual Conversation: Reports from the U.S., U.K., and China." *International Journal of Communication* vol. 9: 1861–1872. Retrieved 5 January 2018 from http://ijoc.org/index.php/ijoc/article/view/3180/1405

Mitchell, Jolyon and Sophia Marriage. (2006). *Mediating Religion: Studies in Media, Religion, and Culture*. London: T&T Clark, p. 288.

National Broadband Plan. (2013). *Doha, Qatar*. Retrieved 24 April 2013.

National Broadband Plan for the State of Qatar. (2013). Dohar, Qatar: Ministry of Information and Communications Technology Qatar, p. 17.

Pavlik, John V., Everette E. Dennis, Rachel Davis Mersey and Justin Gengler. (2013). "Research Plan." *QNRF Research Proposal*. Dohar, Qatar: Qatar National Research Fund.

Reuters. (19 February 2008). "Chronology: From Pigeons to Multimedia Merger." Retrieved 5 January 2018 from www.reuters.com/article/us-reuters-thomson-chronology/chronology-reuters-from-pigeons-to-multimedia-merger-idUSL1849100620080219

Said, Edward. (1978). *Orientalism*. New York: Pantheon Books.

Ulrichsen, Kristian Coates. (2014). *Qatar and the Arab Spring*. London: Hurst.

Weber, Ingmar and Muzammil Hussain and Javier Borge-Holthoefer. (Forthcoming). "Studying Networked Communication in the Middle East: Social Disrupter and Social Observatory." In Sandra Gonzalez-Bailon and Brooke Foucault Welles (eds.), *Handbook of Networked Communication*: Oxford: Oxford University Press.

2 Innovation and media disruption

Introduction

The advent and growth of digital technology have presented the media with an opportunity for a qualitatively distinct type of innovation, what Christensen calls "disruptive innovation." Disruptive innovation potentially brings transformational change. It has the capacity to enlarge or contract the marketplace, adding or subtracting value to the entire system. Therefore, it does far more for consumers and companies than simply adjust the relative position of an individual organization. Disruption may be particularly acute with the rise of mobile and wearable communication technologies.

Fully understanding innovation and media disruption in the context of mobile communications is a multifaceted challenge, rooted in change itself. Communication theorists had long pondered the impact of breaking the time and distance barrier that had constrained human communication and media throughout human history. The trajectory from the first transportable stone tablets to 21st-century mobile devices – such as the laptop and cell phone, not to mention wearable technologies – has given the study of mobile disruptions new currency. This is true not only in the early information societies of Europe, North America and Asia but also markedly so in the Gulf states of the Middle East, the locus of the study reported in this book. Nine out of ten nationals in Lebanon, Qatar, Saudi Arabia and the United Arab Emirates own and use smartphones, and in Qatar and in Saudi Arabia, we find even 1.9 mobile phones per capita (Dennis, Martin, Wood and Saeed, 2017). So smartphones could not be more worthy of study as we ponder their adoption, use and influence in a regional and global economy where disruption, while trailing that of the West, is notable.

While digitization came late to the Gulf states, it took hold quickly, leapfrogging the historical patterns elsewhere – i.e., without having to undergo the long incremental growth of media in the West. There, it dates back to the invention of movable type by Gutenberg, followed by the advance of print and electronic media technologies over nearly six centuries. These media traversed agrarian, industrial and postindustrial societies as a prelude to what has been called the "information" or sometimes "digital" society, now also more and more associated with globalization.

This chapter reviews what research tells us about digital innovation and its implications for understanding mobile-media developments, especially with relevance to them as content platforms.

A theoretical context

Central to the literature about mobile disruptions is the nexus between converging media, especially since the rise of the Internet and the consequences of that *convergence* that led to *disruption*. *Convergence* is the "coming together" of all forms of communication into a single computer-driven system where print and electronic media are blended and accompanied by interactivity, with a capacity theoretically to reach anyone and everyone on the planet. *Disruption*, then, was an assault on that unification, a veritable digital war, aimed at dramatic change or what one media executive meant when he declared that "we aim to break stuff." From the colossus and consolidating impact of Amazon and Google on information, goods and services to such specific applications of disruption as Uber (transport disruption) or Airbnb (lodging disruption), mobile disruption is now central to global communication and an increasingly global economy.

The extent to which classical communication theory applies to this disruption is determined by a dispute that distinguishes *mass* communication from *mediated* communication. Much of communication science and the history of media research is based on media and media audiences as an object of study. The *mass* communication model was drawn from observations of legacy media, such as newspapers, magazines, radio, television and, to some extent, cable. It presumed a communicator sending messages to either an undifferentiated mass audience or to (still fairly large) segments of that audience, defined by demographic characteristics. The advent of digital communication, however, made it possible to communicate with specific individuals in an interactive, multiplatform environment.

This is why some critics challenged the relevance of theories based on media radically different from that of the 21st century. Certainly, *mass* communication still exists, but even those legacy platforms are now wedded to digitization though websites, podcasts and other outlets. Media and mediated communication seem to be replacing the earlier terminology. This may diminish the utility of some mass communication theories such as the two-step flow and perhaps even agenda setting. But few new digitally attuned theories have yet been developed – with the exception of disruption theory itself, clearly a product of the digital age. As we will note later in this chapter, some long-standing theories like the one on the diffusion of innovations, as well as the uses-and-gratifications approach, still have considerable explanatory value (Dennis, 2018).

The history of mass communication and mediated communication research is somewhat contested as scholars seek a (more general) "field theory" supposed to explain the technological component in communication. As thoughtful scholars and critics have demonstrated, there is danger in discarding the basic theoretical building blocks of the communication field, especially if this leans toward technological determinism. Digital disruption does not happen outside of the societal context but rather within it, where many factors and different ways of knowing interact to tell the story of any new technology.

The roots of contemporary literature on digital disruption can often still be traced to basic theories of mediated communication, as well as to the study of cybernetics and quantum mechanics and even to general system theory. The most concerted and focused effort to frame a theory of disruption, however, must be attributed to Harvard Business School Professor Clayton Christensen. His coauthored 1995 article (Bower and Christensen, 1995), "Disruption Technologies: Catching the Wave," in the *Harvard Business Review* was followed by several books, including *The Innovator's Dilemma: When New Technologies Cause Great Firms to Fail* (1997) and *The Innovator's Solution*, with Michael E. Raynor (2003) and by others on leadership, health care and higher education. These writings inspired an avalanche of supportive and critical study. Its results made the term "disruption" popular both in the academy and from Silicon Valley (or Alley or Glen) to Wall Street. Perceived as a "big idea," disruption theory brought its share of challenges and detractors, which are mentioned later in the chapter.

As previously noted, innovation in media has a long but uneven history. Since Gutenberg invented movable type and a practical printing press in Mainz, Germany, in 1450, inventors and innovators have been developing new methods to produce, store, display and distribute content. Whether in the form of print media (books, newspapers and magazines) or broadcast media (television or radio), analog media have seen sweeping technological and economic changes. Publishers, broadcasters, and others introduced a variety of innovations, including the introduction of color in newspapers, three dimensions (3D) in movies, and high-definition broadcasting in television. For the most part, however, these changes were what Christensen calls "sustaining innovations." A *sustaining innovation* refers to incremental change that brings improvement but not reinvention. But, of course, such sustaining innovations may still be sufficient to keep or even expand an individual organization's share of the market.

The advent and growth of digital technology, however, has presented the media with an opportunity for a qualitatively distinct type of innovation, what Christensen calls "disruptive innovation." *Disruptive innovation* brings potentially transformational change. It has the capacity to enlarge or contract the marketplace, adding or subtracting value to the entire system. Therefore, it does far more for consumers and companies than simply adjust the relative position of an individual organization.

What the literature tells us

Christensen's work and that of the institute he founded is the most widely known and cited theoretical and operational foundation for disruption (christenseninstitute.org). It features an explanation of "why disruptive technologies are not breakthrough technologies that make good products better," modularity theory and a theory of hybrids, as well as original work on disruptive *business* models (see Figure 2.1).

There are, however, critics of disruption theory whose studies attack but also clarify and amplify the theory. A particularly searing article by Jill Lepore in *The New Yorker* in 2014 declared disruption to be "a theory of change founded on panic, anxiety and shaky evidence." She complained that the theory had been accepted uncritically and found it inadequate to explain institutional change. Other critics have scored the theory for not sufficiently distinguishing between disruption as a *descriptor* of a process and as a *predictor* of change. Lepore herself was challenged for suggesting that journalism was not subject to disruption.

In his criticism, Ben Thompson (2014) writing in the blog *Stratechery* says that Christensen actually developed two theories of disruption:

1   The **original theory**, now called **new market disruption**, detailed in the original 1997 HBR article and expanded upon in *The Innovator's Dilemma*; and
2   **Low-end disruption,** introduced in a paper called "Disruption, Disintegration and the Dissipation of Differentiability" and detailed in *The Innovator's Solution.*

The first of the two theories explains why incumbent companies ignore new technologies that don't meet their immediate needs or fit their business models. The second offers an integrated model that Thompson thought to be flawed because it seems to work only when a new product is introduced but fails as the market matures. Christensen himself has noted this flaw in the theory, says Thompson, who declares that disruption still "remains an incredibly elegant and powerful theory."

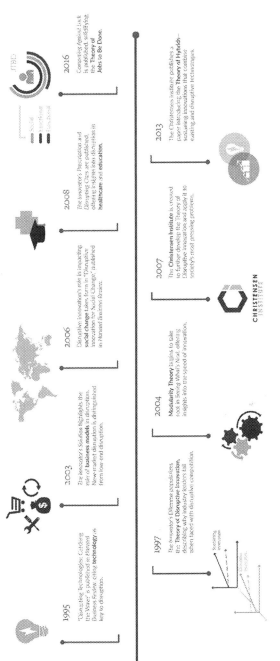

Figure 2.1 The evolution of disruption theory

Source: Christensen Institute

Although the theory has won many converts, another critic, John Linkner, in *The Road to Reinvention* (2014), warns that "fickle consumer trends, friction free markets, and political unrest along with 'dizzying speed, exponential complexity and mind-numbing technology advances mean that a time has come to panic as you've never panicked before.'" Linkner, a venture capitalist and best-selling author, is not a disruption denier. He praises disrupters for shaking up the status quo because they offer their creativity in adapting and improvising in the face of a change that is inevitably driven by the market. Since change is inevitable, Linkner argues that industry leaders, entrepreneurs and even policy makers either drive change by being disrupters themselves or by responding after their enterprises are disrupted.

That a theory predicting radical change should itself have its detractors is no surprise, but the notion of disruption as the successor to the more linear growth in the first phase of the digital revolution still seems a useful explanation of what is happening in the run-up to 2020. Whether the theory is adequate to explain and indeed predict trends in technology and change over a longer period is unknown – because, naturally, no theory is a perfect descriptor or explanatory device in all instances. But disruption has mostly withstood its critics and continues to be widely accepted as the best available explanation for mobile media disruptions. Christensen himself has defended his theory convincingly. As with other theoretical constructs emerging from business schools and tested against a volatile marketplace ("disruption in action"), it is self-evident that disruption theory does not always work in every and all circumstances.

In an effort to focus discussion on how disruptive the development of mobile media per se is, the Spanish scholar C. A. Scolari and colleagues have tried to define and create a taxonomy of contents and applications for mobile media. The authors argue that the digitization of communications has had two phases – the spread of the World Wide Web from the mid-1990s forward, with its massive impact on all sectors of society and the transformation of the Web itself with "the big bang of new mobile devices from smartphones to tablets" (Scolari, Aguado and Feijoo, 2012). This has led to a new standard for mobile communications and media – and especially their content. The "big bang" has been fostered by the flow from cell phones to mobile media devices and from voice to broadband multimedia devices, as well as by an explosive diffusion of mobile applications, the Spanish group says. Content ranges from mobile TV and video to news/information, sports, music, gaming, publishing, advertising and user-generated material. Scolari and colleagues beg off in developing a definitive taxonomy because of the rapid pace of the mobile media market offering new interactive devices, products and applications, any one of which could be a disruptive element in the mobile ecosystem. Media scholar Esther Thorson and colleagues have posited a mobile contingency model that tests how the strength of people's habits using a legacy medium (such as a print or electronic one) can help predict how likely they are to adopt a new medium or application (Thorson, Schoneberger, Karaliova, Kim and Fidler, 2015). Thorson et al.'s "news contingency" model looks for predictors of platform migration depending on various demographics and other factors. This work connects nicely with displacement-and-dependency theory, as well as with uses-and-gratifications theory, collectively guiding our understanding of media adoption and use.

Displacement theory tests whether the adoption of new media displaces the use of older, more traditional media and to what degree. Dependency theory offers a larger template for the degree to which people depend on the media, especially for news and information, but also for personal agenda setting (determining what issues one thinks are important in the public sphere). Uses-and-gratifications theory focuses on the functionality of media, how people relate to them and make use of their content offerings, sometimes for purposes other than the ones intended by the content producers.

In an earlier study, Ester de Waal and Klaus Schoenbach (2010) considered the position of news sites in the media landscape tracking the influence of online media vs. traditional print to see where there was displacement, with readers leaving a medium, vs. complementarity when the audience simply added the new information to its news diet.

Both the penetration of mobile media devices as well as the content people seek out are documented in several media use studies through extensive survey research with large samples. So, for instance, the Pew Research Center, in its annual *State of News Media*, looks at both digital news and advertising patterns in a competitive environment. The University of Southern California's Annenberg School's *World Internet Project Report* does a global survey biannually, which has consistently shown the advance of mobile media use across many consumer functions from home banking to online purchases, with considerable attention to news. Northwestern University in Qatar's annual longitudinal study of *Media Use in the Middle East* has been tracking mobile media use for five years. The studies have documented the rise of social media and use of mobile devices in the aftermath of the Arab Spring. This study focuses on news media in odd numbered years (2013, 2015 and 2017) and on entertainment media in even numbered years (2014, 2016 and tentatively 2018). A companion volume on *Media Industries in the Middle East* was published in 2016. These studies and annual inventories make us aware of how the rapid change in devices and applications challenges research in this arena, which is both fragile and tentative.

The several news-focused studies (previously noted) offer an ambitious agenda for research on media impact. They are consistent in context with John Carey and Martin Elton's *When Media are New: Understanding the Dynamics of New Media Adoption* (2010). Carey and Elton consider how new media are adopted by drawing on Everett Rodgers's theory of the diffusion of innovations. It examines how, why and at what rate new concepts, ideas and technologies spread. While acknowledging the fragility of forecasting, Carey and Elton nevertheless argue that technology history does have value in the accumulation, sorting out and adoption of new technologies, including how platforms change especially with disruptive technologies.

An early digital innovation was the integration of mobile phones into everyday life, disrupting and displacing former institutional and individual routines. This raises questions especially in creative industries concerning whether new ideas are essential to the process of change in the course of economic development, as Gerard Grogin and Larissa Hjorth, 2009) discuss. In a 2011 study, Grogin sought to discover the relationship between the cell phone as a medium and other older forms of media such as TV, radio and print publishing – or such relatively newer forms such as video games. He ponders whether change in media technology also requires a departure from the traditional ways in which we understand their role.

The literature abounds with how specific media functions (news or entertainment) play out in digital media and how they are and can be disrupted. Applying disruptive technology theory drawing on the writings of Christensen, of Bower and Christensen, Tamar Ashuri (2013) reported on how "disruptive innovation" was implemented in a case study of the Israeli newspaper *Yedioth Ahronoth*. Ashuri considered the obstacles that executives faced when they incorporated networked platforms into an "old" medium.

In his study, *Digitizing the News: Innovation in Online Newspapers* (2005), Pablo Boczkowski suggested "that new media emerge by merging existing social and material infrastructures with novel technical capacities, a process that also unfolds in relation to broader contextual trends." He suggests that it is the blending of print media's unidirectional and text-based traditions "with networked computing's interactive . . . and multimedia potentials. The lead author of this volume, John V. Pavlik, has offered both a broad perspective – and specific applications in two pertinent books, *The New Media Technology: Cultural and Commercial Perspectives* (1998) and *Journalism and the New Media* (2001). Pavlik operationalizes the benefits of innovation in new technologies and applies them to the practice of journalism, including conceptualizing, developing and delivering news and information content.

The four domains of media

To track disruption, it is helpful to break down the media ecosystem into four domains:

Content: The key element of content is storytelling, which is true for both established and emerging media.

Distribution: In order for content to be effective, it must get the best possible reach to connect and influence its audiences.

Monetization: As content attracts an audience, that message develops value as it engages and influences.

Audience Building: Through marketing, new forms of content attract audiences, and established forms of content build on their success.

While it is valuable to discuss each of these key factors in isolation, the lines are clearly blurred among them. Some of the best content also functions as great marketing. Distribution provides marketing exposure, as well as insights into producing better content and building greater aggregate audiences. Through monetization, it is possible to create new forms of content, and so on (see Figure 2.2).

In a comprehensive treatment of creative industries, media executive Michael Joseloff's monograph, *Disruption: Digital Innovation and the Entertainment Revolution* tracked disruption across the four domains of media – content, distribution, monetization and audience building. He then focused on the changing face of content (2015, p. 8):

> Content is the substance of media, the story presented to engage and capture the audience. Just as consumer goods companies distribute and sell their core product primarily through retail distributors, so do

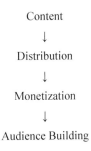

Figure 2.2 The four domains of media

Source: Joseloff (2015)

content creators manufacture their own product and rely on distribution resellers to deliver it to the appropriate audience.

With a focus on seven content areas – news, movies, series, sports and events, gaming, music and radio, he adds specific made-for-digital and made-for-mobile content that can either be original or repurposed from other sources. In this instance and in other treatments of disruption, it is the flexibility and versatility of content that can flow across many platforms, benefitting from the growing convergence and the nuances of disruption that can either impair or even destroy a firm – or give it new life and purpose.

Paul Levinson, in his study of mobile media in *Cellphone* (2004), describes what he calls the "media in motion business" and discusses how portability in media affects content, especially information, once confined to static objects, like books and newspapers. This content can have global reach and influence on the smallest of computer screens in a digital device. The history of photography to which he alludes is one of cameras confined to a studio to those that could be carried almost anywhere, although they were still tethered to darkrooms and fixed-site processing until the arrival of the Polaroid Land Camera. It was to be outdistanced by the early cell phone and eventually by the revolutionary iPhone and its smartphone progeny. They are both platforms for content, including self-generated material, as well as interactive devices enabling the accumulation and distribution of content too.

James Katz has been a pioneer in the study of mobile media with his edited *Handbook of Mobile Communication Studies* (2008). His book, *Mobile Communication: Dimensions of Social Policy* (2011) offers a near encyclopedic treatment of the implications of increased mobile phone use for societies and the issues this generates.

Much of the literature is grounded in modest, systematic efforts to document and chart the impact of digital disruptions while cautiously offering predictive speculation about "the next big thing," as the technology literature refers to a new device or innovation. There is also an historical emphasis with reference to the several generations of technology for wireless communication. For example, as Nelson Granados of Pepperdine University, who covers trends in travel, media and entertainment, wrote in *Forbes* (17 July 2017) that the fifth generation (5G) of technology for wireless communication is anticipated in a two- to three-year period or by 2020 or 2021, citing the Red Chalk Group (see Figure 2.3). He predicts, "I expect nothing less than a disruption in the media and entertainment industry." He argues that the fourth generation (4G) of telecommunications heralded a major change in the way people consume media. Between 2000 and 2010, "[W]e went from a culture

U.S. 5G Rollout Timeline

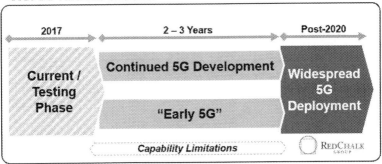

Figure 2.3 U.S. 5G rollout timeline
Source: Red Chalk Group (cited in Granados, 2017)

of downloading content on home computers to a culture of streaming on mobile devices. 4G enabled fast enough streaming capacity for us to enjoy quality content like music and video on our mobile devices." With this backdrop, he predicts that there will be major impacts on content innovation, value chain effects and consumption effects. Red Chalk says 2017 was the testing phase year with continued 5G development and so-called Early 5G, which would lead to widespread 5G deployment after 2020. This is not inconsistent with other futurists who anticipate that increased download speeds will lead to radical innovations in premium content, such as sports and entertainment channels. Of course, many media analysts engage in futuristic speculation, but to some extent this is necessary in surveying the environment for explanatory models and perhaps a generalizable theory media disruption.

The literature of mobile disruption is incomplete, though blessed with a theoretical foundation, even if disputed, of hundreds of studies of mobile media applications and explanatory reports that try to connect this intelligence both with a new media scholarly enterprise and with business intelligence. Understanding what we do know from systematic study rather than mere observation and singular experiences has value in assessing new developments and in making judgments, whether in the academic literature or in business models and plans. Finding a theoretical basis for mobile disruption will no doubt benefit from abstract models and assumptions, as well as from assessments and case studies involving the several communications industries.

References

Ashuri, Tamar. (1 May 2013). "Envisioning the Internet: Implementing 'Disruptive Innovation' in Media Organizations." *First Monday* vol. 18, no. 5.

Boczkowski, Pablo. (2005). *Digitizing the News: Innovation in Online Newspapers.* Cambridge, MA: MIT Press, p. 4.

Bower, Joseph L. and Clayton Christensen. (January 1995). "Disruptive Technologies: Catching the Wave." *Harvard Business Review.*

Carey, John and Martin Elton (2010). *When Media Are New: Understanding the Dynamics of New Media Adoption.* Ann Arbor: University of Michigan Press.

Christensen, Clayton. (1997). *The Innovator's Dilemma: When New Technologies Cause Great Firms to Fail.* Boston: Harvard Business School Publishing.

Christensen, Clayton and Michael Raynor. (2003). *The Innovator's Solution: Creating and Sustaining Successful Growth.* Boston: Harvard Business School Publishing.

Dennis, Everette E. (2018). "Beginnings: Origins of Mediated Communication Research." In Philip Napoli (ed.), *Mediated Communication.* Berlin/Boston: Mouton de Gruyter, in press.

Dennis, Everette E., Justin D. Martin, Robb Wood and Marium Saeed. (2017). *Media Use in the Middle East 2017: A Seven Nation Survey.* Doha: Northwestern University in Qatar. (For earlier surveys in this series that began in 2013, also see Klaus Schoenbach and Robb Wood, with Marium Saeed. (2016). *Media Industries in the Middle East*, Doha: Northwestern University in Qatar (retrieved 19 March 2018 from http://www.qatar.northwestern.edu/docs/publications/research-media-use/2016-middle-east-media-industries-report.pdf) and *Media in the Middle East* (retrieved 19 March 2018 from mideastmedia.org).)

De Waal, Esther and Klaus Schoenbach. (2010). "News Sites Position in the Mediascape: Uses, Evaluations and Media Displacement Effects over Time." *New Media & Society* vol. 12: 477–496.

Granados, Nelson. (17 July 2017). "5G: The Next Tech Disruption in Media and Entertainment Is Coming," *Forbes*, p. 1. Retrieved 5 January 2018 from www.forbes.com/sites/nelsongranados/2017/07/17/5g-the-next-tech-disruption

Grogin, Gerard. (2011). *Global Mobile Media.* New York: Routledge, p. 3.

Grogin, Gerard and Larissa Hjorth, eds. (2009). *Mobile Technologies: From Telecommunication to Media.* New York: Routledge, passim.

Joseloff, Michael. (2015). "Disruption: Digital Innovation and the Entertainment Revolution." Doha: Northwestern University in Qatar, p. 8.

Lepore, Jill. (23 June 2014). "The Disruption Machine, What the Gospel of Innovation Gets Wrong." *The New Yorker.*

Levinson, Paul. (2004). *Cellphone.* New York: Palgrave/St. Martins.

Linkner, Josh. (2014). *The Road to Reinvention.* San Francisco: Jossey Bass, passim.

Pavlik, John V. (1998). *The New Media Technology: Cultural and Commercial Perspectives.* New York: Allyn and Bacon.

Pavlik, John V. (2001). *Journalism and the New Media.* New York: Columbia University Press.

Scolari, Carlos A., Juan M. Aguado and Claudio Feijoo. (April 2012). "Mobile Media: Towards a Definition and a Taxonomy of Contents and Applications." *iJIM* vol. 6, no. 2: 29.

Thompson, Ben. (18 June 2014). "Critiquing Disruption Theory." *Stratechery*.

Thorson, Esther, Heather Schoneberger, Tatsiana Karaliova, Eujin Kim and Roger Fidler. (2015). "News Use of Mobile Media: A Contingency Model." *Mobile Media & Communication* vol. 3, no. 2: 160–178.

3 Mobile media

Introduction

Fueling disruptive change in the media marketplace in Qatar and the Gulf region is the development of network-enabled mobile media technology. Internet-connected, smartphones and tablets have ushered in a wide range of possibilities for innovation in the realm of digital media content creation, design, distribution and access. In June 2013, Nielsen reported that three in five, or about 60%, of mobile subscribers in the United States had smartphones (Nielsen, 2013). Northwestern University in Qatar's (NU-Q) multination survey investigation, launched in 2013, found that mobile penetration is even greater in the Middle East. In the countries NU-Q studied, about 70% of people use smartphones and 22% use tablets (Dennis, Martin, Wood and Saeed, 2016). Moreover:

> From 2013 to 2016, Internet penetration rose in all six countries surveyed, but most dramatically in Egypt, as well as Lebanon. Internet penetration in Tunisia stagnated over the past few years and is the lowest among countries surveyed. Nearly all nationals in Arab Gulf countries use the internet.
>
> (p. 10)

Further, "Large majorities of the populations in Gulf countries have mobile broadband access."

Poised for even further change in the mobile arena is a new generation of wearable digital devices, such as head-worn, Internet-enabled devices including smart watches, augmented reality eyewear, and virtual reality head-worn displays such as the Samsung Galaxy Gear introduced in 2013, the Oculus Rift introduced in 2016, and Google Daydream View introduced in 2017.

Research on digital media innovation has thus far largely focused on the business of media, especially the funding models and revenue structure for organizations. Studies of media innovation have tended to examine how traditional enterprises can adapt to the networked, digital environment in terms of building profitable, sustainable business or funding models. Some research has contrasted and compared these traditional enterprises' adaptive experiences with so-called digital first ventures, efforts designed to create a digital-only product or one that delivers first digital content that can be repackaged for analog media. The central research questions have revolved around revenue strategies, such as paywalls for digital news products or evolving advertising models based on auctions, the viability of strategies for content purchase and subscription in the networked environment, or strategies for monetizing user-generated content, social media and data mining. Some studies have examined the nature and characteristics of innovators themselves and what fosters a greater adoption tendency and successful media innovation (Frambach and Schillewaert, 2002). Others have examined the nature of interorganizational networks and technical innovation (Fu, Cooper and Shumate, 2017). Few studies of media innovation have focused on content and how entrepreneurs might reinvent this basic building block of media and how that reinvention might influence engagement with the public (Khan and Richards, 2013).

This gap in the research literature on media innovation and engagement has been particularly pronounced in the realm of mobile media content. The research literature on mobile media content innovation and engagement has been even more scant in Qatar, the Gulf and the Middle East and North Africa (MENA) region. Much of the research to date has concentrated on infrastructure and not content (Arab Advisors, 2013a, 2013b). Here we provide research on content uniquely designed for mobile distribution, consumption and user engagement in Qatar and the Gulf that has been almost nonexistent. Gunter and Dickinson (2013) have examined the state of news media in the Arab world, including in the Gulf region.

In developing a framework for this research, which aims to investigate mobile media content innovation from the consumer and industry perspectives, there is a considerable body of both theoretical and applied study in the adoption and diffusion of innovations. Most fundamental is the pioneering work of social science scholar Everett M. Rogers (1962, 1983, 2003) who has contributed three essential bodies of research to the literature: the process of innovation, influences on the rate of adoption of innovation and the categories of adopters of innovation.

Rogers's seminal work, *Diffusion of Innovations*, outlined the process through which innovations (both products and ideas) are ultimately adopted or rejected by either individuals or organizations. Rogers outlined five stages in the process of adoption of an innovation: (1) knowledge, (2) persuasion, (3) decision, (4) implementation and (5) confirmation.

In stage one, potential adopters become aware of an innovation but lack insufficient information to make a decision. In stage two, potential adopters become interested in the innovation and seek information about it. In stage three, potential adopters evaluate the advantages or disadvantages of an innovation, ultimately making a decision. In stage four, the adopter implements a trial of the innovation, assessing the overall usefulness of the innovation. In the final stage, the adopter confirms the utility of the innovation and uses it more extensively.

Research by Rogers indicates that at least five factors influence the rate of adoption of an innovation: (1) the perceived relative advantage of the innovation, (2) compatibility, (3) complexity or simplicity, (4) trialability and (5) observability.

Rogers also identified five categories of adopters of innovations. In general, as shown in Figure 3.1, research demonstrates that early adopters of an innovation, called "innovators," constitute about 2.5% of all potential adopters of an innovation. These individuals or organizations are likely to become advocates for the innovation. They facilitate category two, early adopters, and are about 13.5% of the population. Category three, early majority adopters, comprise about one-third, or 34%, of the population. Category four, late majority adopters, comprise about one-third, or about 34%. Category five are laggards or late adopters and are the final 16% of the population.

We have employed this five-factor model in the current research to identify the impediments to the potential adoption of mobile media innovations. These form a core part of in-depth interviews with leaders at innovative media enterprises in Qatar and the Gulf and will be integral to the case studies we present in Chapter 6, as well as to our analysis of consumer adoption and use of mobile media forms and content as presented in Chapter 4 where we discuss the findings of surveys conducted in Qatar and the United Arab Emirates (UAE).

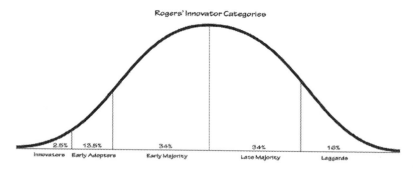

Figure 3.1 Adopters of innovations

Source: Rogers. (2003). *Diffusion of Innovations*, 5th ed. New York: Free Press

The research of Rogers and others more recently (e.g., Garrison, 2001; Wisdom, Chor, Hoagwood and Horwitz, 2013) on the adoption and diffusion of innovations is highly relevant to the introduction of mobile media innovations in Qatar, the Gulf and the Middle East and North Africa (MENA) region more broadly. This body of work suggests a framework for understanding the nature and rate of adoption of innovations in media, including mobile media content.

Tully (2015) has further refined the application of Rogers's model in a contemporary mobile media environment. In an international study based in Kenya, her study focuses on how organizations make decisions regarding the adoption of information and communication technology (ICT). In particular, her article looks at organizations in Kenya and their use of or rejection of a new mobile media application, the Ushahidi Platform (2017), an open-source software system designed for digital content development including mobile media content development, especially in an international context.

She found some confirmation of earlier research regarding the work of Rogers and others that identified five technology attributes as central to an organization's evaluation of an emerging innovation. Importantly, she revealed that certain attributes, including perceptions of trialability and observability, play a more pronounced role in assessing a technological innovation. Moreover, she provided evidence for a new attribute, perceived flexibility, as increasingly important especially in assessing evolving mobile media technologies. This is at least in part due to the nearly continuous development of mobile media, including software and related apps, which perform a variety of functions including some related to content format and substance. For instance, an update might improve the mobile device privacy, security or geolocation capacity important to augmented reality.

Based on Rogers's categories of adopters of innovation and related research, we identified a set of Qatar-based media industry organizations who are early adopters of mobile media. Among these are Firefly Communications, publishers of *The Edge* and other media, as well as iLoveQatar. net, and the Al Jazeera Media Network. These mobile media early adopters served as integral to case studies in mobile content innovation in this research investigation. We have worked with them to investigate public engagement with their use of mobile media. In this form, the research builds "bridges between businesses, government, academia, and other stakeholders in Qatar, and between Qatar and the international research community" (QNRF, 2013, p. 4). Notably, these partnerships build "collaboration between academic stakeholders and nonacademic stakeholders inside Qatar" (p. 4).

Content innovation strategies

To conduct this investigation, we developed a multidisciplinary conceptual framework of content innovation strategies for mobile, digital media. This model builds on the prior media studies work of Pavlik, who has developed a framework identifying strategies for content innovation in digital media generally (Pavlik, 2007). Pavlik's general digital media content innovation model posits that two basic dimensions characterize digital media content. One dimension is the extent to which the content has been created for or is original to digital media distribution and presentation. In industry parlance, this is called "digital-first." On one end of the spectrum is repurposed content, content that was created originally for analog media distribution, such as print formats (newspapers, magazines or books) or audio/visual media formats (radio, television or motion pictures).

The second dimension is the extent to which the content has been designed or optimized for the digital environment and the unique capabilities it affords. Drawing upon the work of Feiner and others in computer science (Feiner, Macintyre and Seligman, 1993), we know that on one end of the designed-for-digital spectrum is content designed for traditional, analog media and that on the other end is content specially designed to utilize the features and functions unique to the digital, networked and increasingly mobile environment. Examples of content designed for the digital environment are web links, social media capabilities or multimedia. Farther toward the horizon are immersive, interactive and multisensory formats such as augmented reality, mixed reality and virtual reality.

Figure 3.2 summarizes this model of innovation strategies for digital content. Type I refers to content designed for analog media and then repurposed to a digital platform. This is the lowest level of digital content innovation. Type II refers to content original to digital media but still designed for the capacities and characteristics of analog media. Type III refers to repurposed content but adapted to a digital design, such as adding links to linear text

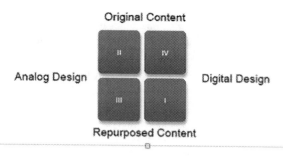

Figure 3.2 Strategies for digital content innovation

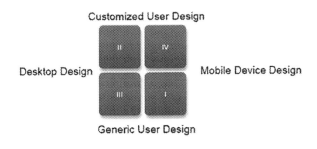

Figure 3.3 Content innovation strategies for mobile, digital media

created originally for print media. Types II and III represent a moderate level of digital content innovation. Type IV refers to content that is both original to the digital environment but also optimized for the qualities or capabilities unique to digital platforms.

Building on this model, we have developed for this research project a new model for content innovation strategies for mobile, digital media. This model is summarized in Figure 3.3.

In this model, we have identified four types of content, combining the notions of user customization and device mobility. Type I is digital content designed for desktop computers at fixed, network-enabled locations but without any user customization. Type II is desktop designed but features user customization of content, such as content adapted to user preferences. Type III content does not feature user customization but is optimized for the capabilities unique to mobile, digital media. Type IV combines both user customization and mobile device design capabilities.

Type III – generic content for desktop computers – is perhaps the most frequently created content, whether text, audio, photos, graphics or video. Types I and II – generic content for mobile and user-customized content for desktop computers – are increasingly being created.

Type IV is the rarest form of mobile media content, but it is on the ascent in terms of production, distribution and audience engagement in many parts of the world. It is not only customized for the user but is optimized for a mobile platform. This comprises a set of five dimensions summarized in Figure 3.4. These dimensions help to differentiate mobile, digital media from the traditional, analog print media of newspapers, magazines and books. Analog print media may be highly mobile (it is easy to pack a magazine in your carry-on to read on the plane, for example), but these media lack the qualities featured in these five dimensions. Type IV, mobile and user-optimized, content, builds on what is called responsive design (Marcotte, 2010). Responsive design content is fluid and optimized for easy reading, viewing and listening across a range of devices. Second, Type IV content supports and integrates user interactivity and networked capacity for two-way communication and thereby supports the contributions of user-generated content (UGC). Content is thus shareable in a social media, many-to-many model rather than one-to-many. Third, Type IV content is intelligent, dynamic, and adaptable. It provides not only updates but also location-aware and user-customized, contextualized presentation.

Fourth, Type IV features the convergent modalities of sight, sound and moving pictures or video, as well as a tactile user interface. It is increasingly three-dimensional (3D) and built for wearable display. It is increasingly featuring immersive or enveloping forms of content, including 360 photos and video, spatial audio and haptic or tactile media experiences.

Fifth, it offers functionality and heightened user control.

Summarizing the model in Figure 3.4, Type IV content is mobile and user-optimized with five dimensions or qualities:

1 **Responsive design**: Fluid, ease of user experience
2 **Interactive:** Many –to-many, supports UGC
3 **Intelligent:** Dynamic and adaptable, location-aware
4 **Convergent:** Sight, sound, haptic, 3D
5 **Functional:** User –controlled, and actionable

An example of Type IV content is the situated documentary, a type of immersive journalism using augmented reality (AR). Developed by Höllerer, Feiner and Pavlik, the situated documentary provides a multimedia narrative on handheld or wearable devices in which content is geometrically registered with the real world (Höllerer, Feiner and Pavlik, 1999). Depending on the user's location and orientation, multimedia content is overlaid virtually onto real-world objects and locations viewed or otherwise experienced

Dimension	Qualities
1. Responsive Design	Fluid, ease of user experience
2. Interactive	Many to many, supports UGC
3. Intelligent	Dynamic and adaptable, location-aware
4. Convergent	Sight, sound, haptic, 3D
5. Functional	User controlled and actionable

Figure 3.4 Type IV content: mobile and user-optimized

through mobile media. GPS data are used to track the user's position. Augments, or virtual messages, are presented when the user is in a position to most effectively experience that augmentation.

The user experiences an AR enhancement displayed on his or her mobile device, such as a 3D image, overlaid onto a real-world scene that is seen, heard, or felt through the handheld or wearable display. Through an intuitive, natural user interface (NUI) design, the user controls navigation through the story content. By gazing at an interactive object, such as a virtual color-coded flag, the user can access layers of content such as video, audio or graphics. Prototypes of situated documentaries feature a variety of story themes such as past events that occurred on the campus of Columbia University where the research was conducted.

In the years since the development of the situated documentary form, commercial technologies have been developed that bring consumer-friendly mobile and wearable media forms into the increasing mainstream. Consequently, a growing number of media organizations, including news media such as *The New York Times*, *USA Today*, the British Broadcasting Corporation (BBC), *The Guardian*, and the Associated Press (AP) have developed reporting and storytelling in news coverage via AR and VR (virtual reality). A growing number of media enterprises in the Middle East, including Qatar and the Gulf, have developed such experiential media efforts as well. These include Al Jazeera, whose efforts we discuss in Chapter 6 (Al Jazeera, 2017).

Previous research demonstrates the substantial and growing use of mobile devices in Qatar and the Gulf region more broadly. Data in fact have shown that mobile phone penetration per capita is greater in Qatar than in any other country in the world, at 2.79 mobile devices per person (CIA *World Fact Book*, 2012). This is followed by the UAE (2.27), with Saudi Arabia at number 11 (with 1.79), Libya at number 14 (1.72) and Kuwait at number 17 (1.63). Although these mobile cellular penetration rates do not include tablet or other mobile devices (e.g., e-readers), adoption rates for tablet devices are growing significantly in the Middle East as well. The International Data Corporation (IDC) reports that the size of the tablet market exceeded that of the mobile PC market in the Middle East and Africa for the first time during the second quarter of 2013 (IDC, 2013). Tablet shipments were up more than 200% for the year, at a total of 2.79 million units (IDC, 2013).

On 7 October 2013, Northwestern University in Qatar hosted its second meeting of the Media Industry Forum (NU-Q, 2013). Included on a panel at the Forum were speakers from ILoveQatar.net, Agency 222, the Supreme Council of Information and Communication Technology (ictQatar), and the Pan Arab Research Center. Panelists described the Qatar media as in transition from the world of analog to digital, including broadband and mobile.

Khalifa Al Haroon, founder of ILoveQatar, declared that the future of media in Qatar is digital. Hussein Fakhri, CEO of Agency 222, presented preliminary research results of Agency 222's Qatar Thinks survey titled "State of the Net." The survey showed that 92% of respondents in Qatar access the Web on a daily basis. Velislava Metodieva, researcher at ictQatar, provided additional evidence of the growing digital media in Qatar, reporting that the Web presence of businesses in Qatar has doubled and that social media is fast becoming the preferred method for government institutions to reach their public.

Data from NU-Q's survey of media use in eight Arab nations in the Gulf, Levant and MENA region, begun in 2013 and continued through 2017, confirm the digitization of Qatar media content as well (MENA Media Survey, NU-Q, 2013, 2014, 2015, 2016, 2017). Qatar nationals in particular are digitally connected, relying on online sources for news and information to a greater extent than any other medium, except television. Eighty-five percent of Qatari nationals use the Internet, as compared to 87% who watch television. The percentage of Qataris who use the Internet significantly exceeds those who listen to radio (67%) or read newspapers (63%), books (43%) or magazines (31%). Significantly, more than nine out of ten (91%) of Qataris who go online report using the Internet through wireless handheld devices. The largest portion of the mobile devices used by Qataris is the smartphone (84%), followed by tablets (49%) and laptop computers (46%). Qataris are also heavy users of social media, with 67% of Qataris using social media and spending an average of 3.9 hours per day on social networking sites. The most popular social networking sites among Qataris are Facebook (65%) and Twitter (65%), followed by Instagram (48%) and Google+ (9%).

Although we do not know the direction of causation, this preliminary consumer evidence correlates with the emergence of early efforts to deliver content via mobile media that is potentially optimized for that media platform. Several Qatar-based media enterprises have introduced mobile media apps, including DohaNews.com, the *Gulf Times* and the Al Jazeera Media Network.

Importantly, data on the public's use of digital and especially mobile media to access the Internet suggest there is a strong consumer foundation for mobile media content innovation Qatar and the Gulf region generally. A 2016 NU-Q MENA survey provides data on mobile media usage in Qatar and the Arabian Gulf region. A vast majority (84%) of Qatari nationals use a smartphone, with nearly half (49%) using tablets. A majority (76%) of Arab expats similarly use smartphones but are less inclined (only 32%) to use tablets. Levels of mobile media usage are lower still among Asian and Western expats but still sizeable.

Mobile media are transforming traditional forms of public communication and on multiple levels. Around the world, including Qatar and the Gulf region, mobile media platforms have grown tremendously in the 21st century. By mobile media, we are referring to handheld or wearable digital communications devices that are networked and thereby provide Internet access and direct person-to-person communication capacity, as well as increasingly mass communication capability. In fact, around much of the world including Qatar and the Gulf, such mobile media have become increasingly the dominant platform for both interpersonal and mass communication. Increasingly, persons in much of the world, including Qatar and the Gulf, are engaged for ten or more hours a day on their mobile media platforms.

These platforms include a variety of devices, including smartphones, laptop computers, tablets, MP3 players and wearables, including smart watches, fitness trackers and the like. Head-worn devices are beginning to grow in consumer adoption and usage as well. Smartphones are the leading platform for most consumers and mediated communication. While traditional media forms are still important, they are declining in usage relative to mobile media, especially among younger consumers (Pew, 2016). Consumers still read printed newspapers, magazines and books and watch digital television sets and listen to radio.

Video is among the most extensive forms of media production, distribution and consumption in the Arab world. As noted by Khalil (2016, p. 120):

A total of 134 unique high-definition (HD) channels are targeting the Arab world using four satellites: Arabsat (42), Nilesat (29), YahLive (27), and Noorsat (12) – channels available on special set-top boxes (24) . . . . Of these channels, 71 are provided free, making the HD offered in MENA higher than the total HD offered in Italy, Spain and Russia combined. By February 2014, the total satellite HD channels constituted around 11% of the total satellite channels aired in the Arab World. HD TV channels have increased by 30% from 2013 to 2014. Unlike the US and UK operators, Arab pay-TV operators are not up-selling their HD content – except for sports channels. This recent interest in HD channels prompted a UAE-based company, My-HD, to offer 34 channels of which 19 are HD . . . . Saudi Arabia and the UAE together accounted for 75% of total My-HD subscriptions at the end of 2013 – followed by Qatar (with 12% of total subscriptions), Kuwait and Iraq (4% each).

But increasingly citizens access the content produced for these platforms via their mobile devices. Moreover, traditional media organizations are designing and producing content intended for distribution via and consumption on mobile media. As our data show, this trend is true in Qatar and the Gulf and increasingly all around the world.

Moreover, also as reflected in our data, social media have grown tremendously in their use and increasingly on mobile platforms. Again, this is as true in Qatar and the Gulf as it is around the world.

Other research confirms these patterns (Pew, 2017). Katz (2017) reports on a national survey regarding the interest level in virtual reality and immersive media delivery. This investigation looked at U.S. attitudes concerning immersive media and their ability to substitute for travel. This study indicated there was not strong interest in such technology.

References

Al Jazeera. (9 May 2017). "Al Jazeera to Host Summit on the Future of Media." Retrieved 26 May 2017 from www.aljazeera.com/indepth/features/2017/05/al-jazeera-host-summit-future-media-170509082754703.html

Arab Advisors. (2013a). "New Arab Advisors Group Report: An Overview of Qatar National Broadband Network." Retrieved 5 January 2018 from www.access-arabadvisors.com/report/view?id=2867

Arab Advisors. (2013b). "Qatar Launches Mobile Number Portability Service." Retrieved 5 January 2018 from www.access-arabadvisors.com/report/view?id=2535

CIA *World Fact Book*. (2012). "Country Rank for Mobile Cellular Per Capita." Retrieved 5 January 2018 from www.indexmundi.com/g/r.aspx?v=4010

Dennis, Everette E., Justin D. Martin, Robb Wood and Marium Saeed. (2016). *Media Use in the Middle East 2016: A Six-Nation Survey*. Retrieved 7 August 2017 from www.qatar.northwestern.edu/docs/publications/research-media-use/2016-middle-east-media-use-report.pdf

Feiner, Steven, Blair Macintyre and Doree Seligmann. (1993). "Knowledge-Based Augmented Reality." *Communications of the ACM* vol. 36, no. 7: 53–62.

Frambach, Ruud T. and Niels Schillewaert. (February 2002). "Organizational Innovation Adoption: A Multi-Level Framework of Determinants and Opportunities for Future Research." *Journal of Business Research* vol. 55, no. 2: 163–176.

Fu, J. Sophia, Katherine R. Cooper and Michelle Shumate. (2017). "Use of Information and Communication Technologies (ICTs) in Nonprofit Collaboration: An Exploratory Study." International Communication Association Annual Conference.

Garrison, Bruce. (August 2001). "Diffusion of Online Information Technologies in Newspaper Newsrooms." *Journalism* vol. 2, no. 2: 221–239.

Gunter, Barrie and Roger Dickinson, eds. (2013). *News Media in the Arab World: A Study of 10 Arab and Muslim Countries*. London: Bloomsbury Publishing.

Höllerer, Tobia, Steven Feiner and John Pavlik. (18–19 October 1999). "Situated Documentaries: Embedding Multimedia Presentations in the Real World." Proc. ISWC '99 (Third International Symposium on Wearable Computers), San Francisco, CA, pp. 79–86.

IDC. (2 September 2013). "MEA Tablet Market Surpasses Portable PC Market for First Time, IDC Says." Retrieved from http://www.thetechstorm.com/2013/09/idc-middle-east-africa-tablet-market-surpasses-portable-pc-market-for-first-time/

Katz, James. (4 April 2017). Email communication with Pavlik.

Khalil. Joe. (2016). "The Future of Television: An Arab Perspective." In John V. Pavlik (ed.), *Digital Technology and the Future of Broadcasting: Global Perspectives*. Abingdon/New York: Routledge, pp. 109–123.

Khalil, Joe F. and Marwan M. Kraidy. (2009). *Arab Television Industries*. London: Palgrave BFI. 978-1-84457-576-3.

Khan, Muqeem and Sandra Richards. (2013). "Kinesthetic Learning System for Arabic Indigenous Dances." QNRF Grant NPRP No.: 6-364-5-030.

Marcotte, Ethan. (25 May 2010). "Responsive Web Design." *A List Apart*. Retrieved 20 March 2017 from https://alistapart.com/article/responsive-web-design

Nielsen. "Mobile Majority: U.S. Smartphone Ownership Tops 60%)." Retrieved from http://www.nielsen.com/us/en/insights/news/2013/mobile-majority-u-s-smartphone-ownership-tops-60-.html

Pavlik, John V. (2007). "Developing Media Content Strategies for the Digital Age." *Zitimata Epikinonias (Communication Issues)* vol. 5, no. 1: 9–26.

Qatar National Research Fund (QNRF). (2013). "Request for Proposals (RFP) for the National Priorities Research Program (NPRP)." QNRF: Dohar, Qatar.

Rogers, Everett M. (1962). *Diffusion of Innovations*. Glencoe, IL: Free Press; Rogers. (1983). *Diffusion of Innovations*, 3rd ed. New York: Free Press; Rogers. (2003). *Diffusion of Innovations*, 5th ed. New York: Free Press.

Tully, Melissa. (2015). "Investigating the Role of Innovation Attributes in the Adoption, Rejection, and Discontinued Use of Open Source Software for Development." *ITI Journal* vol. 11, no. 3: 55–69. Retrieved 1 July 2017 from http://itidjournal.org/index.php/itid/article/view/1423

Ushahidi. (2017). Retrieved 1 July 2017 from www.ushahidi.com/

Wisdom, Jennifer P., Ka Ho Brian Chor, Kimberly E. Hoagwood and Sarah M. Horwitz. (2013). "Innovation Adoption: A Review of Theories and Constructs." *Adm Policy Ment Health* vol. 41, no. 4: 480–502. DOI: 10.1007/s10488-013-0486-4

4 Mobile media in Qatar and the Gulf

Introduction

In this chapter, we report the preliminary results of one facet of a multi-method research investigation in Qatar and the UAE. We provide evidence drawn from the first two rounds of surveys of public usage of mobile media in Qatar conducted in 2016 and 2017 and in 2017 in the United Arab Emirates (UAE). These surveys are part of a larger research design that includes a four-part approach. It is a study funded by the Qatar National Research Fund.

Reported first here are the initial findings from a multiyear survey of mobile Internet users in Qatar and the UAE to assess their engagement – and the experiences associated with that engagement – with content on mobile media apps. These data are based on samples of approximately 600 persons in each country in each of two years. Reported in Chapter 6 are the results of a second part of the study, a series of in-depth case studies of innovative media organizations in Qatar and the Gulf region to identify their adoption of content innovation strategies for mobile media. Reported in Chapter 5 are the results of a third part of the study, a test, in a quasi experimental design, of content innovation strategies currently in use or under development by the media organizations featured in stage two of this research.

This multipart research examines strategies and adoption patterns for mobile media content innovation, particularly in Qatar and the UAE. The investigation provides a data-driven model of potential mobile media content innovation in these countries, including both production and consumption patterns and a translational framework for mobile media innovation strategies and an assessment of "best practices" in mobile media content in the region. Particular attention is given to users' engagement with content designed for mobile media, including journalism and emerging experiential formats such as augmented reality (AR) and virtual reality (VR).

The central research questions that guide this discussion are the following, with individual hypotheses stated with regard to data gathered in Qatar and the UAE:

1   **Data-driven:** What mobile media content innovation strategies create consumer-level engagement, particularly in Qatar and the UAE?

    a   To what extent do consumers prefer content formats optimized for mobile devices, including content customization, multimedia, interactivity, geolocation and augmented reality on mobile platforms, particularly in Qatar and the UAE?

        i   H1: User engagement will be highest for content optimized for digital, mobile platforms and user customization, particularly in Qatar and the UAE.

        ii   H2: User engagement will be lowest for content optimized for neither the user nor mobile device, particularly in Qatar and the UAE.

        iii H3: User engagement will be moderate for content optimized for either user or mobile device, particularly in Qatar and the UAE.

    b   What factors influence consumer adoption of mobile media innovations in Qatar and the UAE? Do these reflect the factors identified by Rogers and others?

    c   What is the rate and pattern of consumer adoption of mobile media innovations in Qatar and the UAE? Do these patterns mirror the rates of innovativeness identified by Rogers and others?

In this chapter, we present data gathered to address these research questions and hypotheses. Subsequently, in Chapter 6, we examine data we have collected concerning the following research questions:

2   **Best practices:** What lessons emerge from an analysis of current mobile media innovation in Qatar and the Gulf region?

    a   Which media in Qatar and the Gulf region have developed unique mobile media content?

    b   To what extent do consumers prefer these mobile-optimized media content experiences?

    c   To what extent do the five stages of adoption and diffusion of an innovation apply to mobile media innovation in Qatar and the UAE more broadly?

d   To what extent do the five factors that influence innovation adoption operate with regard to mobile media innovation adoption in Qatar and the UAE more broadly?

e   To what extent are the five types of adopters of an innovation reflected in those media enterprises that adopt mobile media innovation in Qatar and the UAE more broadly?

3   **Fueling the next generation:** What steps will ensure that mobile media innovation characterizes the next generation of media leadership in Qatar and the UAE?

a   What standards, practices and policies are most likely to facilitate adoption of mobile media innovation strategies?

b   What obstacles remain to the adoption and diffusion of strategies for mobile media innovation in Qatar and the UAE?

We also examine the implications of this research with regard to the development of mobile media in Qatar and the UAE and potentially the entire Gulf region. This research can help to advance the understanding of consumer preferences for content on mobile media. Importantly, this research provides an overview of the current state of innovation in the mobile media arena in Qatar and the Gulf. This baseline allows us to assess over time the development of innovation in mobile media in the region.

Finally, this research can help to build human capacity for mobile media innovation in Qatar and the Gulf and do so ethically and responsibly. This research can help to achieve these ends in at least three ways. First, through the research, we develop and test innovative content strategies for mobile media that can continue to be utilized in mobile media endeavors. Second, the lessons learned in the research can help develop curricular innovations in journalism and media education programs. This can help improve the education of students in the use of innovative content approaches to mobile media in Qatar and the region. Finally, the partnerships engaged in the research can help those media enterprises develop their own ongoing strategies for content innovation. Taken as a whole, this research can make for a lasting contribution to sustainable and ethical economic growth and development in Qatar and the region.

Research design and methods

As outlined in Figure 4.1, the multi-method research design we have developed follows a three-year timeline. In Year 1, we began with a quantitative evaluation of consumers' engagement and potential adoption of mobile

Year 1: Consumer engagement with and adoption of mobile media content innovation (quantitative survey)

Media industry leadership development of mobile media content innovation (in-depth interviews)

Year 2: Qualitative testing of consumer engagement with specific mobile media content innovations (defined in Year 1)

Consumer engagement with and adoption of mobile media content innovation (quantitative survey begun in Year 1 and social media consumer-level data)

Year 3: Next-generation entrepreneurial training for mobile media content innovation

Consumer engagement with and adoption of mobile media content innovation (quantitative survey begun in Year 1 and social media consumer-level data)

Figure 4.1 Three-year investigation of mobile media content innovation

media content innovation in Qatar and the UAE. We extend this data collection across all three years of the study, but we present evidence only from the first two years in this book, as we are writing these words at the end of calendar year 2017, and Year 3 data collection will not occur until 2018. We also are conducting qualitative evaluation of media industry leaders' strategies for the adoption of mobile media content innovation in Qatar and the Gulf region. We present the findings of this part of the investigation in Chapter 6.

In Year 2, we have conducted a qualitative and quantitative exploration of the effect of specific mobile media content innovations (defined in Year 1) on consumer engagement and continued quantitative evaluation of consumers' engagement and potential adoption of mobile media content innovation in Qatar and the Gulf region.

In Year 3, we will explore the facilitation of the next generation of entrepreneurs' adoption of mobile media content innovation via educational opportunities; this will be the final year of quantitative evaluation of consumers' engagement and potential adoption of mobile media content innovation in Qatar and the UAE. Although this book does not include the findings from Year 3, the overall design provides important context for the entire investigation.

Complementary to the multiyear and multicountry survey of consumers, the study design includes gathering data from public, social media sources including Twitter, Facebook, Instagram, Google+ and YouTube for postings related to user experiences with local mobile media content and analyzing those data using social network analysis (Rosenthal and McKeown, 2011). In this part of the study, we have monitored geolocated social media including Twitter, Facebook, Instagram, Google+ and YouTube for mobile media postings associated with locally produced mobile content in Qatar and the UAE and the Gulf region generally. By tracking and analyzing these posts, we offer insight on the role of local mobile media in customers' daily lives. And while customers who are socially active on mobile media may represent only a segment of the population, they are at the center of the target for potential adoption of local media for mobile.

We evaluate geographically tagged mobile and social media messages to develop a location-based assessment of UGC patterns and mobile media usage in the region. We present findings from this analysis in Chapter 7.

Independent and dependent variables

The independent variable in this investigation is the extent to which mobile content is optimized for both the mobile device and the user, including customization based on preferences and characteristics, as well as location and other context.

The dependent variable in this investigation is user engagement. User engagement is defined by the strength of the underlying experiences users have with media. In addition to measuring experiences, we will collect data about time spent with various mobile media and content applications. Research suggests time spent is a reliable and valid method of collecting data about digital media usage (Mersey, Malthouse and Calder, 2010). We will also examine interaction with the content (e.g., clicking on embedded links) and related use of social media (e.g., using Twitter to share short text messages related to the content, posting related photos on Instagram, sharing related information Facebook).

Survey design and sampling plan

Collecting time-series data enhances the value of this research in that we are able to capture changes in both media innovation and consumer adoption across time and throughout the Gulf region. Across all years of the study, we have worked with a Qatar University–based research organization, the Social and Economic Survey Research Institute (SESRI, 2017), to draw our consumer sample, design the survey instrument and conduct the interviews via telephone.

Sampling utilizes list-assisted dialing based on a comprehensive sampling frame provided by a telecommunications company in Qatar. List-assisted sampling is a technique used in telephone surveys. It utilizes information from a mobile telephone frame and directory listings to produce a simple random sample. It is simpler than and as effective as other methods of respondent selection such as the next-birthday technique (Salmon and Nichols, 1983). The UAE survey has been contracted through IPSOS (2016), a local survey institution based in Dubai, UAE. IPSOS has conducted a corresponding telephone survey based on its own proven sampling frame but using the same survey instrument. We have created a Mobile Media Use survey for this investigation. Copies were developed in English and Arabic. Institutional Review Board (IRB) review and approval for the project have been provided by multiple IRBs, including that of Rutgers and Georgetown–Qatar. Human subject protections for this study include an English-language copy of the informed consent form as well as an Arabic-language version we developed for and used in the study.

The international dimension of this research has presented unique challenges beyond the need to secure IRB approval from three different institutions in two different countries. Because this study involves data collection in Qatar and the UAE, combined with the election of President Donald Trump in the United States in 2016, this study has taken on new, perhaps unprecedented complications in data collection. In particular, in early 2017, five Gulf nations, including the Kingdom of Saudi Arabia and the UAE, formally broke off diplomatic relations with Qatar. Twitter and other communications from President Trump were referenced in the context of this diplomatic maneuver, with Trump alleging that the State of Qatar supports terrorism at the highest levels (Wintour, 2017). In addition, the five Gulf states that have broken off diplomatic ties with Qatar (not the first time, but this time seems especially tense) have also demanded that Qatar close down the Al Jazeera Media Network, which is part of this study. Further, the five Gulf nations have imposed a trade embargo on Qatar, which, as of this writing, depends on Turkey for the import of food and other goods. Qatar is home to a major U.S. air force base, used to fight terror in Yemen, and is also home to a new military base of Turkey.

Such conditions make conducting research in the region especially challenging. Coauthor Gengler (2015) faced similar challenges in gathering survey data for his doctoral dissertation in Bahrain. The conditions require methodological nimbleness and adaptability to the conditions as they shift politically and on the ground.

President Trump has also issued an executive order restricting travel to and from the United States and some countries in the region. Further, the Department of Homeland Security in the United States in early 2017 banned laptops as carry-ons on planes flying via Qatar Airways to the United States. Although some travelers might not object to placing their laptop in checked luggage, the Lead-PI on this project does, and therefore he did not bring his laptop on flights to Qatar until the ban was officially lifted later in 2017. Such travel restrictions complicate completing work tasks. With only a mobile phone available for much of the trip and the need to rely on only computers already in place in his hotel in Doha and at NU-Q, writing and data analysis became especially challenging.

Not only are the U.S-based research team members required under the parameters of the grant-making organization (QNRF) to visit Qatar twice annually as part of the research, but the research process involves contracting with the Dubai-based research firm to collect data twice a year in the UAE.

The survey was conducted among the general population 18 years and older in two countries in the Gulf: Qatar and the UAE. Sampling in each country includes nationals and expatriates. We have chosen these two countries as representative of the Gulf region and in part representative of the previous NU-Q MENA survey. Across the two countries, we are seeking a total of 4,800 respondents to complete the survey (at least 600 in each country, or 1,200 total in each of the three years, about 300 Qatari and UAE nationals and 300 expatriate professionals, or roughly 600 total in each of the three years), although only Years 1 and 2 data for Qatar and Year 1 for the UAE are reported in this book. Year 1 fieldwork was conducted between December 2016 and May 2017 in the two countries. The survey was conducted via telephone in Qatar and the UAE. The survey was offered in Arabic or English, depending on the respondent's language preference. Before conducting first-year fieldwork, we undertook a small-scale pilot test of the survey instrument.

The survey took about 10–15 minutes to complete, depending on language (i.e., the Arabic language version tended to take slightly longer than English as some phrasing requires more words). The questionnaire consists of approximately 50 questions or response items, focusing primarily on the measurement of the independent and dependent variables, including demographics and mobile media usage and content interest. We measure mobile media usage in terms of time spent. The questionnaire includes items related to subject demographics and other background information, as well as items that measure mobile media usage. We designed the questionnaire during the first half of Year 1 of the study, 2016.

Also in 2016, we conducted in-depth interviews with 50 media industry leaders in Qatar and the Gulf region to assess interest in or adoption of mobile media innovations. Chapter 6 presents detailed analysis and description of these organizations' mobile media products and strategies. We use these materials to provide detailed case studies of mobile media content innovation in Qatar and the Gulf region.

For our industry leadership interviews, we have drawn upon the Media Industry Forum roster developed by NU-Q, as well as NU-Q partner organizations. The media industry leadership will include Qatari-owned and -controlled media properties: ILoveQatar.net and *The Edge* business magazine.

Each of these has a digital, mobile presence or is developing one. We also study DohaNews.com, a wholly digital enterprise that in 2013 launched a mobile app optimized for mobile media use, the *Gulf Times*, as well as regional media with mobile apps, including satellite video provider OSN (Orbit Showtime Network).

In addition to understanding the strategy and status of mobile media content innovation within their organizations, these interviews also addressed these leaders as early adopters. We will assess their adoption stage:

1   **Knowledge**, the extent to which adopters are aware of mobile media content innovation strategies and to what extent they have insufficient information to make a decision
2   **Persuasion**, the extent to which innovators are interested in mobile media content innovation and seek information about it
3   **Decision**, the extent to which adopters evaluate the advantages or disadvantages of an innovation, ultimately making a decision
4   **Implementation**, the extent to which innovators implement a trial of mobile media content innovation, assessing the overall usefulness of the innovation, or
5   **Confirmation** of mobile content innovations, the extent to which innovators confirm the utility of the innovation and use it more extensively

In-depth interviews also queried these leaders in terms of (1) the perceived relative advantage of mobile media content innovation, (2) compatibility, (3) complexity or simplicity, (4) trialability and (5) observability.

Year 2

In the second year of the project, we focused on evaluating the effects of mobile media content innovations identified in Year 1 on consumer engagement. We worked with regional media industry leadership identified in Year 1 to both update our case studies begun in Year 1 and to test user response to content optimized for mobile media and user customization. We have used two means of consumer testing. We report on these in Chapter 5.

The execution of the first, quasi-experimental design testing of the effects of mobile media content innovation is highly dependent on the findings from Year 1. Based on what we learn about the mobile media products already deployed or in development, we will design a randomized block study to qualitatively test the use and effect of these products. It may be that we are able to iteratively test products currently being developed, but we will most certainly focus on, at least in part, products that are already live to the consumer. Details of this part of the study and related findings are presented in Chapter 5.

In the third year of the project, we will focus on evaluation of the expanse of qualitative and quantitative data collected to identify mobile media content innovations that drive engagement. In Year 3, we will also conduct the final phase of our three-year, longitudinal data collection through the Mobile Media Use survey. Year 3 fieldwork will be conducted in 2018 in Qatar and the UAE. We will analyze the time-series consumer engagement data with attention to innovative developments across time, changing behavior and attitudes, country-to-country differences and regional attributes, but unfortunately due to the time parameters of this book's publication cycle, we cannot include these results in this book.

Findings: results of Year 1 and Year 2 survey of mobile media use in Qatar

Following is a summary of the findings from our survey of public usage of mobile media in Qatar in Year 1 and Year 2. Data on sample size are provided in Tables 4.1 and 4.2. This provides a basic description of how the public is using mobile media in Qatar, an introductory comparison of similarities and differences between mobile media usage among Qatari nationals

Table 4.1 Sample size frequency (*N*) in Qatar, Year 1, 2016

Country	Frequency	Percent	Cumulative
Qatar	317	52.83	52.83
Arab	193	32.17	85.00
Non-Arab	90	15.00	100.00
Total	600	100.00	

Table 4.2 Sample size frequency (*N*) in Qatar, Year 2, 2017

Country	Frequency	Percent	Cumulative
Qatar	319	48.63	48.63
Arab	254	38.72	87.35
Non-Arab	83	12.65	100.00
Total	656	100.00	

and expatriate nationals, and an initial test of the central research question of this study, that the public will engage particularly with content designed for mobile media platforms.

All results are disaggregated by survey year and by respondent social category (Qatari, Arab expat, non-Arab expat) in order to make sense of the results and to afford bases for valid comparisons. This is especially important in light of demographic changes in Qatar between the Year 1 and Year 2 surveys owing to the blockade, namely the increased representation of Arab expats in the non-Qatari sample. All results utilize probability sampling weights that account for survey design effects. The data are weighted for sampling probability, so the proportions are somewhat different from those based on the actual N.

Following is a descriptive summary of the results of the Year 1 and Year 2 Mobile Media Use survey. We also include a comparison of the results between Qatari nationals and expatriate professionals. Finally, we offer an initial analysis of the findings with regard to the central research question of the study, that public engagement will be heightened with content optimized for mobile media platforms.

For each item, we provide a brief textual summary of the findings from the survey. We include tabular results for the key survey items, especially as they relate to mobile media content usage and interest in tables in the text. These data tables include a key to the reading of the data, frequencies and column percentages.

RESPONDENT SUMMARY

As the data in Table 4.1 indicate, in Year 1 we completed interviews with a total of 600 respondents in Qatar, including roughly half (53%) Qatari nationals and half (47%) expatriates, including (32%) Arab professionals and (15%) non-Arab professionals. As Table 4.2 shows, in Year 2 we completed interviews with a total of 656 respondents in Qatar, including roughly the same patterns as in Year 1, with about half (49%) Qatari nationals and about half (51%) expatriates, including Arab expatriate (39%) and non-Arab expatriate professionals (13%).

DEMOGRAPHIC PROFILE

To establish the basic characteristics of the sample and its general representativeness of the broader population, we begin with a demographic description of the sample. In this discussion, we provide a verbal description of the data and any notable differences between Years 1 and 2, but the precise percentages and numbers are generally provided in these tabular data.

In terms of gender, slightly more than half in both years are male, and less than half are female. Among Qatari nationals, in both Years 1 and 2, just more than half are males, and almost half are female. Likewise across both years, about two-thirds of the Arab expatriate professionals and non-Arab expatriate professionals are male, and about a third are female.

In terms of marital status, most (more than two-thirds in both years) are married (about 72% Years 1 and 2). The portion of Qatari nationals married is slightly lower (about 65% Years 1 and 2). Small portions are never married, divorced, or did not respond. There is great diversity among the expatriate respondents in terms of their country of nationality and birth, including United States, UK and India. Similarly, the age of respondents varies widely in both Year 1 and Year 2 from about 20 years to persons in their seventies. In Years 1 and 2, about 22% are between 25 and 34. Thirty-seven percent are between 35 and 44. Eleven percent of respondents are between 45 and 54, and 11% of respondents are 55 or older. Mean age in both years is 37 years, with little variation among groups.

There is also diversity in terms of education, with college education being the largest portion. Expatriates have a slightly higher level of education with about half having a college degree, compared to just under a third of Qatari nationals, who are slightly more likely to hold a secondary degree.

Household size also varies widely in the sample. Qatari nationals tend to live in larger households than expatriate professionals surveyed. Expatriates tend to live in households with one (27%) or two persons (45%) in Years 1 and 2. In both years, about a third (34%) of Qatari nationals live in households with one or two persons. Two-thirds live in larger households.

Most respondents in both years are employed (70%), with expatriates employed at a slightly higher rate than Qatari nationals (76% compared to 64%).

Household income levels are higher among Qatari nationals than expatriate professionals in both years. In both years, about half (53%) of Qatari nationals report monthly income of 50,000 QR or more. About half (53%) of the expatriates report a monthly income of less than 25,000 QR. With a U.S. dollar conversion rate of about 3.74 QR to $1.00, this converts to about $6,700.

MOBILE MEDIA USAGE

Data show that, among those surveyed, mobile media usage is almost universal. We asked respondents, "Thinking about yesterday, how many hours did you spend using a mobile device?" In both years, just 2% said they did not use a mobile device on the prior day, with little difference between Qatari nationals and expatriate professionals (3% of Qatari nationals, 2% of Arab and non-Arab expats in both years). In both years, more than a quarter reported using a mobile device for five or more hours in the prior day, with little difference between Qatari nationals and expatriate professionals.

In both years, only a third of Qataris and Arab expats used a laptop, while more than half of non-Arab expats did so. Most used a handheld mobile device. Typically, this is a smartphone. About a fifth of Qatari nationals used a tablet, compared to a slightly greater percentage of Arab expats and even more non-Arab expats. Few used an e-reader (such as a Kindle). Slightly more of all groups (about a tenth) used an MP3 player (for music).

Time spent using mobile devices was high, especially a smartphone. In both years, almost nine of ten used a smartphone for an hour or more in the prior day. Highest usage is among Arab expats, followed by Qataris and non-Arab expats. More than half used a smartphone for more than two hours the day before, about the same for both Qataris and Arab expats and slightly fewer among non-Arab expats. More than a quarter used a smartphone for more than five hours the day before, with the percentage increasing by a third from Year 1 to Year 2 among Qataris but not among expatriates. These data suggest smartphone use is rising among Qataris but not among expatriates.

Tablet usage was not quite as high. Half of Qataris (49% Y1, 47.3% Y2) reported using a tablet in the prior day an hour or less. Non-Arab expats had even lower usage, with more than half (56.6% Y1, 74.1% Y2) reporting using a tablet an hour less in the prior day. Arab expats reported somewhat higher usage, with just a third (33.2% Y1, 43.4% Y2) reporting using a tablet an hour or less in the prior day and about two-thirds using it an hour or more.

Internet usage is high in all groups. Almost a third (32.5% Y1, 36.9% Y2) of respondents reported using the Internet for five or more hours in the prior day (similar levels among all groups, Qataris, Arab expats, non-Arab expat professionals).

Those studied reported using the Internet for at least a decade, with the average number of years of Internet usage exceeding ten for all groups (10.8 Y1, 11.2 Y2 for Qataris, 10.1 Y1 and 10.8 Y2 for Arab expats, and 11.1 Y1 and 12.8 Y2 for non-Arab expats).

The number of years respondents have used a mobile device to access the Internet is substantial, though not quite as long as Internet usage overall. The average number of years a mobile device has been used for Internet access is 6.9 in Y1 and 7.5 in Y2 overall (similar for all three groups).

When asked about their use of a mobile device in the prior day to access the Internet, fewer than one in ten (about 8% in Y1 and Y2) said they did not do so. In Year 1, a quarter (26%) said they used their mobile device to access the Internet in the prior day for less than an hour at home (about the same for all groups), while just a fifth (20.6%) reported so in Year 2. Half (50.6% Y1, 51.1% in Y2, similar across all three groups) said they used their mobile device to access the Internet for more than two hours in the prior day at home. Use of mobile devices to access the Internet at work or school was slightly lower at both Year 1 and Year 2 across all three groups, though still substantial, with more than a third using their mobiles to go online more than two hours in the prior day.

As to what type of Internet content is accessed in the prior day via their mobile device, about two-thirds (71.3% Y1, 71.2% Y2) said they accessed news and information. This broke down to nearly two-thirds (63.1% Y1, 70.8% Y2) of Qatari nationals, compared to three-quarters (77.7% Y1, 69.5% Y2) of Arab expatriates and slightly fewer (70.3% Y1, 76.5% Y2) of non-Arab expat professionals.

About half (48.5% Y1, 51% Y2) said they used their mobile device in the prior day to watch a movie or video (similar for all groups).

The vast majority in Years 1 and 2 of all groups said they used their mobile device to access or engage social media in the prior day. Nearly one in ten said they did so for five or more hours, with Qataris especially apt to do so. About a fifth said they used their mobile device in the prior day to play a game (similar for all groups). A third said they used their mobile device for audio content (music or podcast) in the prior day (slightly more Qatari nationals, compared to a third of Arab expats and a quarter of non-Arab expats). About one-tenth said they used their mobile device in the prior day to read an e-book: more Qatari nationals than Arab expats or non-Arab expats.

Privacy is a very high concern when using a mobile device. In both years, two-thirds are somewhat or very concerned. Likewise, more than two-thirds of non-Arab expats share this concern. Hackers are the main concern (nearly three-quarters, with much lower percentages concerned about tracking by family or friends and companies and government surveillance). Differences between groups are limited, with non-Arab expats somewhat more concerned about government surveillance and tracking by companies, while fewer Qataris and Arab expats share these concerns.

In terms of social media mobile apps, respondents indicated a high level of usage. Nearly all (96% Y1 and Y2) said they used their mobile device to access a social media app in the prior day.

Qatari nationals were active on Twitter, with about half using it to share short text messages with other users. Moreover, among Qataris, Twitter use in the prior day is on the rise from Year 1 to Year 2, compared to just a fifth of Arab expat professionals and even fewer non-Arab expats. Most Qataris also reported using Instagram, especially for sharing photos and videos, compared to less than half of Arab expats and even fewer non-Arab expats. Snapchat, a visual app with augmented reality, was a Qatari national favorite, with nearly three-quarters reporting using the app in the prior day, compared to just a fifth of Arab expats and even fewer non-Arab expats using it. YouTube was popular among all groups, with nearly three-quarters indicating they used the YouTube app in the prior day.

About a quarter of all groups (29.9% Y1 and 25.7% Y2 overall with relatively little differences between groups) said they used Google+ in the prior day.

Expatriates had a clear preference for Facebook, with more than eight of ten indicating they used the Facebook app on their mobile device in the prior day. Less than a fifth of Qatari nationals used the Facebook app in the prior day.

LinkedIn was less popular in general, with one in ten having used the app in the prior day across Years 1 and 2. Even fewer used the Flickr, Tumblr, or reddit apps.

Regarding mobile media app usage, the specific content app used varied considerably depending on the particular group. Mzad Qatar (online classified advertising) was the most used overall, with one-fifth in both years having used their mobile app in the prior day to access the app. Mzad Qatar's primary audience is Qataris; nearly a quarter used it via their mobile app. Similarly, Arab expats accessed it in the prior day via their mobile device more than any other mobile content app studied. In contrast, very few non-Arab expats used their mobile device to access the Mzad Qatar app in the prior day.

Al Jazeera was the most used news mobile app overall, with almost one-fifth in both years accessing the app via their mobile device in the prior day. Usage was relatively even across all three groups in both years. DohaNews was popular among all groups, with more than one in ten accessing the app in the prior day. But it was especially popular among expatriates, with highest rates among non-Arab expats and Arab expats, compared to less than one-tenth of Qataris using the Doha news app the prior day. About a third of non-Arab expats accessed the QatarLiving app in the prior day, compared to one-fifth of Arab expats and just one in 20 Qataris.

Just one in 20 in both years overall used their mobile device in the prior day to access the *Gulf Times* app. But one-tenth of non-Arab expats did so, compared to almost no Arab expats or Qataris. About one-tenth of each group used their mobile device in the prior day to access the ILoveQatar app. About one in 20 of all groups accessed the OSN app in the prior day.

A small percentage of all groups in both years accessed the online shopping app Namshi.

Relatively few reported being aware of the emerging mobile media content format called augmented reality (AR). AR is a technology that uses a mobile device to overlay video, graphics and audio onto things seen or heard in the physical world through a mobile device's camera. Less than a tenth Qataris (4.8% Y1, 8.1% Y2) and Arab expats (7.0% Y1, 8.2% Y1) said they were familiar with AR, although the percentage grew from Year 1 to Year 2. More than 10% (13.9% Y1, 10.1% Y2) of non-Arab expats said they were familiar with AR.

Table 4.3 Q15a. Interest in augmented reality (AR) in Qatar, Year 1

	Qatari	Arab expat	Non-Arab expat	Overall
Very interested	13.8%	15.9%	20.2%	16.3%
Somewhat interested	27.4%	34.7%	26.4%	30.3%
Not very interested	14.8%	9.3%	14.0%	12.2%
Not at all interested	31.1%	27.0%	26.0%	28.0%
Don't understand it*	12.9%	13.1%	13.4%	13.1%

*Final option was volunteered by respondents.

Table 4.4 Q15b. Interest in augmented reality (AR) in Qatar, Year 2

	Qatari	Arab expat	Non-Arab expat	Overall
Very interested	14.7%	14.4%	22.7%	16.1%
Somewhat interested	27.9%	38.4%	35.5%	34.8%
Not very interested	11.1%	9.1%	10.0%	9.9%
Not at all interested	32.8%	28.8%	18.0%	27.9%
Don't understand it*	13.5%	9.3%	13.9%	11.4%

*Final option was volunteered by respondents.

In both years, about half of all surveyed in all groups said they would be somewhat or very interested in AR if it were available. Details are in Tables 4.3 (Q15a) and 4.4 (Q15b).

AR can also be embedded into real-world objects, such as buildings, statues, and the like, and accessed by the user via a mobile device pointed at or in proximity to the object. More than half of all groups in both years expressed interest in using AR via their mobile device if AR content were embedded into real-world objects in Qatar. It is worth noting that among every group surveyed, interest in embedded AR in Qatar is growing to now well over half the population. Details are in tabular data Q16a and Q16b.

Pokémon Go is a mobile game that uses AR, and when introduced to the global marketplace in 2016, it not only caused something of an international sensation in mobile game play; it also brought AR to relatively widespread public attention in many parts of the world. Respondents in our survey were prompted, "Please tell me how interested you are in playing Pokémon Go." About a fifth (9.5% Y1, 9.0% Y2) of all groups said they would be somewhat or very interested in playing Pokémon Go if it were available in Qatar.

Across both years, more than half of all groups said it would be somewhat or very likely that they would share their AR experiences via social media.

Less than a quarter of Qataris, just under a third of Arab expats, and more than a third of non-Arab expats have heard of the emerging mobile media technology called virtual reality (VR).

VR can employ a wearable device such as a headset like Google Cardboard or the Oculus Rift or HTC Vive headset to immerse users in 360-degree or spherical photos, video or computer animation. In both years, more than half of those surveyed of all groups said they would be somewhat or very interested in experiencing VR. This includes about half of Qataris, almost two-thirds of Arab expats, and just over half of non-Arab expats. Details are in Tables 4.5 (Q19a) and 4.6 (Q19b).

Nearly two-thirds of all surveyed in both years said they would be somewhat or very likely to share their VR experiences via social media including more than half of Qataris, two-thirds of Arab expats, and more than half of non-Arab expats.

Gender and age differentials may play a potentially important role in mobile media usage. Socioeconomic position and educational differences are also relevant as well. These are dimensions we will include in the analysis of our complete data set for all three years of the study.

Overall, the findings reported in this chapter provide clear though preliminary evidence that Qataris and expatriate professionals, Arab and non-Arab

Table 4.5 Tabular data: Q19a. Interest in virtual reality (VR) in Qatar, Year 1

	Qatari	*Arab expat*	*Non-Arab expat*	*Overall*
Very interested	15.9%	20.3%	25.4%	20.2%
Somewhat interested	29.6%	40.2%	28.7%	33.9%
Not very interested	11.7%	11.6%	15.3%	12.6%
Not at all interested	32.7%	21.5%	24.4%	25.7%
Don't understand it*	10.2%	6.4%	6.3%	7.6%

*Final option was volunteered by respondents.

Table 4.6 Tabular data: Q19b. Interest in virtual reality (VR) in Qatar, Year 2

	Qatari	*Arab expat*	*Non-Arab expat*	*Overall*
Very interested	17.4%	20.5%	37.6%	22.9%
Somewhat interested	32.6%	38.7%	29.5%	35.1%
Not very interested	8.8%	9.7%	9.0%	9.3%
Not at all interested	30.0%	26.7%	11.1%	24.7%
Don't understand it*	11.3%	4.4%	12.8%	8.0%

*Final option was volunteered by respondents.

alike, have a strong interest in content formats designed for mobile media platforms. More than half expressed interest in AR and VR experiences. They also expressed strong interest in sharing AR and VR experiences via social media.

Results of Year 1 survey of mobile media use in the UAE*

Following is a report of the findings from the Year 1 survey of public usage of mobile media in the United Arab Emirates. This preliminary report provides a basic description of how the public is using mobile media in the UAE, an introductory comparison of similarities and differences between mobile media usage among Emirati nationals and expatriate nationals, as well as an initial test of the central research question of this study, that the public will engage particularly with content designed for mobile media platforms. A second round of interviews in the UAE was conducted in fall 2017 but is not included here. These interviews were conducted during the trade embargo and may have been affected by the tensions surrounding this period. We are still examining these data for their reliability and validity, and we expect to report these findings at a future date.

Method

The method used in the UAE parallels that used in Qatar. To assess public engagement with mobile media content, we conducted a survey of a randomly selected sample of adult media consumers in the UAE to establish a baseline measurement of use of engagement with and interest in mobile media content innovations. Our sampling frame includes adults, both Emirati nationals and members of the expatriate communities. The Year 1 survey is the first phase in a three-phase (or three-year) design.

For all three years, the Qatar-based research organization (SESRI) designed the consumer sample and assisted in the design of the survey instrument. However, data collection in the UAE is by an independent commercial research firm based in the UAE. We have contracted with Dubai-based IPSOS to conduct the interviews via telephone. Sampling utilizes list-assisted dialing based on a comprehensive sampling frame provided by a telecommunications company in the UAE.

As in Qatar, the UAE survey took about 10–15 minutes to complete, depending on language. Likewise, the questionnaire consists of approximately 50 questions or response items, focusing primarily on the measurement of the independent and dependent variables as well as demographic information. We measured mobile media usage largely in terms of time spent

and frequency of use and interest in content designed for mobile media platforms. Total sample size is 609, with data collection in April and May 2017.

Findings

A descriptive summary of the results of the Year 1 Mobile Media Use survey in the UAE follows and includes a comparison of the results between
Emirati nationals and expatriates. Finally, we offer an initial analysis of
the findings with regard to the central research question of the study, that
public engagement will be heightened with content optimized for mobile
media platforms. We follow this discussion with a comparison of the patterns observed in the UAE with those seen in Qatar.

For each item, we provide a brief textual summary of the findings from
the survey. We follow this with a comparison to findings from the same
survey instrument as utilized in Qatar.

Respondent summary

We completed interviews with a total of 609 respondents in the UAE,
including mostly expatriates (n = 541, or 89%) with about one-tenth Emirati
nationals (n = 68, or 11%).

Demographic profile

To establish the basic characteristics of the sample and its general representativeness of the broader population, we begin with a demographic description of the sample.

In terms of gender, almost three-quarters (73%) of those surveyed are
male, and about a quarter (27%) are female. Among UAE nationals, about
two-thirds are male (66%), and about a third are female (34%). Nearly
three-quarters (73%) of the expatriate professionals are male, and about a
quarter (27%) are female.

Concerning marital status, two-thirds of those surveyed are married
(65%). The portion of Emirati nationals married is slightly lower (60%) and
expats slightly higher (66%), although this is not a statistically significant
difference. Small portions are never married, divorced, or did not respond.

Among the respondents, there is great diversity among the expatriates
in terms of their country of nationality and birth, including United States,
UK and India. Similarly, the age of respondents varies widely from about
20 to the sixties. About half (43%) are between 25 and 34. A quarter (24%)
of respondents are between 35 and 44. Eleven percent of respondents are
between 45 and 54, and four% are 55 or older.

There is similar diversity in terms of education, with college education being the largest portion (42%). Emiratis surveyed have a slightly lower level of education with about half (57%) having a college degree, compared to almost six in ten (58%) expats surveyed.

Household size also varies widely in the sample. Emirati nationals tend to live in larger households than expatriates surveyed. Most (94%) Emirati nationals live in households with three or more persons. Eighty-eight percent live in households with four or more persons. Two-thirds (71%) of expatriates live in households with two or more persons. About a quarter (29%) live in single-person households.

Most respondents are employed (77%), with expatriates employed at a slightly higher rate than Emirati nationals (78% compared to 68%).

Household income levels are higher among Emirati nationals than expatriates. About half (47%) of Emirati nationals report monthly income of 40,000 AED or more (AED-to-US $ conversion is about 4:1). About a third (29%) of the expatriates report a monthly income of 15,000 AED or less.

Approximately 45% of those surveyed have a single cell phone, but 38% have two.

Mobile media usage

Data show that among those surveyed, mobile media usage is almost universal. We asked respondents, "Thinking about yesterday, how many hours did you spend using a mobile device?" About 1% said they did not use a mobile device in the prior day, with little difference between Emirati nationals and expatriates (1% of Emirati nationals, 1% of expats). More than a third (35%) of Emiratis reported using a mobile device for more than five hours in the prior day, while among expatriates four in ten (40%) did so.

Emiratis and expats alike used a variety of mobile devices to access the Internet, including laptops, smartphone, tablets, e-readers and MP3 players.

About a quarter used a laptop (28% of UAE nationals and 27% of expats). Most used a handheld mobile device. Typically, this is a smartphone (93%, almost the same for both Emirati nationals and expats). Less than a fifth used a tablet (slightly more Emirati nationals, 15%, than expats, 11%). Few (1–2%) used an e-reader (such as a Kindle). Slightly more (about 8%) used an MP3 player (for music).

Time spent using mobile devices, especially a smartphone, was high. About three-quarters used a smartphone for an hour or more (similar among UAE nationals, 78%, and expats, 74%). More than half used a smartphone for two or more hours (about the same for both groups: 58% of Emiratis, 53% of expats). About a quarter used a smartphone for five or more hours (22% of UAE nationals, 22% of expats).

Among those with a tablet, usage was not quite as high. Twelve percent of Emiratis reported using their tablet for an hour or more in the prior day. About six percent of expats reported using their tablet in the prior day for up to an hour or more.

Internet usage is high among those surveyed. Most (88%) respondents reported using the Internet for at least an hour in the prior day (similarly high among both groups).

More than half (51%) report having used the Internet for at least a decade.

Two-thirds (66%) report they have been using a mobile device to access the Internet for five or more years (similar among both groups).

When asked about their use of a mobile device in the prior day to access the Internet, none said they did not do so. About half (53%) said they used their mobile device to access the Internet in the prior day for an hour or more (almost all for Emiratis).

As to what type of Internet content they accessed in the prior day via their mobile device, more than half (56%) said they accessed news and information: half (50%) of UAE nationals, compared to more than half (56%) of expatriates.

About half (49%) said they used their mobile device in the prior day to watch a movie or video (similar for both groups).

The vast majority (92%) of both groups said they used their mobile device to access or engage social media in the prior day. About one in ten (13%) said they did so for five or more hours. A fifth (about 22%) said they used their mobile device in the prior day to play a game (similar for both groups). A fourth (28%) said they used their mobile device for audio content (music or podcast) in the prior day (slightly more Emirati nationals, 31%, compared to a quarter of expats, 27%). About one-tenth (11%) said they used their mobile device in the prior day to read an e-book (slightly more Emirati nationals, 13%, than expats, 10%).

Privacy is a very high concern when using a mobile device. Nearly two-thirds (60%) of those surveyed are somewhat or very concerned (similar among both groups). Hackers are a major concern (40% overall), with the next highest concern tracking by family members or other relatives (6%) ahead of government (2%) or corporate (4%) surveillance.

In terms of social media mobile apps, respondents indicated a high level of usage. Nearly all (99%) said they used their mobile device to access a social media app in the prior day (similar among both Emiratis and expats).

UAE nationals were active users of Instagram (a heavily photo-based app), with nearly half (46%) using the app in the prior day, compared to just a fifth (19%) of expats. A third (33%) of Emiratis also reported using Snapchat. Snapchat is a visual app in which photos disappear after being received and viewed. In addition, Snapchat offers users the capacity to overlay augmented reality onto photos. Just 10% of expats reported using Snapchat in the prior day. A fifth (22%) of Emiratis reported using Twitter (mostly to share short text messages) in the prior day, compared to 6% of expats. Facebook was favored by expats (38%), compared to just a tenth (12%) of Emiratis. YouTube is popular among both groups, with more than a third of (35%) Emiratis indicating they used the YouTube app in the prior day and a quarter (27%) of expats.

Less than a tenth (about 8%) of both groups used Google+ in the prior day.

LinkedIn was less popular among Emiratis (about 4% used the app in the prior day) than among expats (8%). Even fewer used the Flickr, Tumblr, or reddit apps.

The vast majority of both groups (97%) used their mobile to access content from the Al Jazeera app, *Gulf News* app, 7Days app, *Khaleej Times*, dubizzle, or Namshi. High usage patterns were similar for both groups.

Few reported being aware of the emerging mobile media content format called augmented reality (AR). More than nine in ten (95%) said they were unfamiliar with AR (similar among both groups, slightly fewer 7% of Emiratis). AR is a technology that uses a mobile device to overlay video, graphics and audio onto things seen or heard in the physical world through a mobile device's camera. Nearly half (42%) of both groups (35% of Emiratis, 51% of expats) said they would be somewhat or very interested in AR if it were available.

AR also can be embedded into real-world objects, such as buildings, statues, and the like. About half of both groups (50%) expressed interest in using AR via their mobile device if AR content were embedded into real-world objects in the UAE.

With regard to Pokémon Go, a mobile game that uses AR, we asked those surveyed, "Please tell me how interested you are in playing Pokémon Go." Few in either group said they would be interested in playing Pokémon Go if it were available in the UAE (14% of expats, 4% of Emiratis).

About half (50%) of both groups said they would be interested in sharing their AR experiences via social media.

Just under a third (28% of Emiratis, 29% of expats) have heard of a new mobile media technology called virtual reality (VR).

VR uses a wearable device such as a headset like Google Cardboard or the Oculus Rift headset to immerse users in 360-degree or spherical photos, video or computer animation. More than one half (55% of Emiratis, 57% of expats) of both groups say they would be somewhat or very interested in experiencing VR. More than half (62% of Emiratis, 58% of expats) of both groups said they would be interested in sharing their VR experiences via social media.

These findings provide clear though preliminary evidence that Emiratis and expatriates in the UAE alike have significant interest in content formats designed for mobile media platforms. More than half express interest in AR and VR experiences. They also express strong interest in sharing AR and VR experiences via social media.

Comparing Qatar and the UAE

Comparative demographic profile

On most demographic variables, the profiles between the Qatar and UAE samples are similar. In terms of marital status, most are married in both samples, whether nationals or expatriates. Age varies widely in both samples and across expat and national groups. In both samples, there is substantial diversity among the expatriate professionals in terms of their country of nationality and birth.

There is also diversity in terms of education in both samples, with college education being the largest portion. Household size also varies widely in both samples. In both samples, most respondents are employed. Likewise, in both samples household income levels are higher among nationals than among expatriates.

There are two notable differences in the demographic profiles of the Qatar and UAE samples. In terms of gender, while slightly more than half (61%) are male in the Qatar sample, about three-quarters are in the UAE sample. This difference is true across nationals and expatriates groups. The UAE sample also contains a significantly higher portion of expatriates than nationals, as compared to the Qatar sample, which is balanced. We control for or test these differences in our analysis.

Comparative mobile media usage

In both samples, the data show that among those surveyed, mobile media usage is almost universal. Likewise, the dominant mobile platform, in both samples, and for Qataris, Emiratis and expatriates, is the smartphone.

In both samples and across all groups, time spent using mobile devices was high, especially using a smartphone.

Similarly, Internet usage is high among all groups in both samples. About two-thirds of all groups and both samples report having used the Internet for at least a decade.

Most in both samples and all groups also report they have been using a mobile device to access the Internet for five or more years.

One area where a difference in mobile media emerged is when respondents were asked about their use of a mobile device in the prior day to access the Internet. In Qatar, fewer than one in ten said they did not do so, and a quarter said they used their mobile device to access the Internet in the prior day for less than an hour (about the same for both groups). About half of those in the UAE survey said they used their mobile device to access the Internet in the prior day for an hour or more (almost all for Emiratis).

Another difference emerged when respondents were asked about what type of Internet content they accessed in the prior day via their mobile device. In Qatar, about a two-thirds said they accessed news and information, for both Qatari nationals and expatriates. Mobile news consumption is slightly lower among those in the UAE survey. Just over half said they accessed news and information in the prior day on their mobile device, among both Emiratis and expats.

About half of all groups and both samples said they used their mobile device in the prior day to watch a movie or video.

While the vast majority of both groups said they used their mobile device to access or engage social media in the prior day, those in the Qatar sample were even more likely (nine of ten vs. eight of ten).

Among respondents in both samples and across national and expat groups, privacy is a very high concern when using a mobile device.

In terms of social media mobile apps, respondents in both samples and across all groups indicated a high level of usage. There are differences in the samples as to which mobile social media apps used. Qatari nationals were active on Twitter, while UAE nationals were the heaviest users of Instagram. Among expats in both samples, Facebook was the most used. However, in Qatar, nearly nine of ten expats used it via their mobile device in the prior day, while less than half those in the UAE did so.

Respondents in both samples and across all groups used a variety of news apps, although use of any individual news app was relatively low in the Qatar sample. Preferred news apps include the Al Jazeera app, DohaNews, and Qatar Living, especially among Qatari expats. In the UAE sample, respondents across all groups were apt to use, via their mobile, the *Gulf News* app, 7Days app, *Khaleej Times*, dubizzle, or Namshi.

With regard to emerging immersive mobile media content forms, few respondents in both samples reported being aware of augmented reality (AR). Yet, in both samples and across all groups, nearly half said they would be somewhat or very interested in AR if it were available. Likewise, about half of those in the Emirates and those in Qatar said they would be interested in using AR to explore cultural or other objects located in their respective countries. Those interviewed in both samples expressed relatively little in interest in playing Pokémon Go, which is a mobile game that uses AR.

Still, about half of those in both samples and all groups said they would be interested in sharing their AR experiences via social media.

About a third of those surveyed in both samples have heard of an emerging mobile media technology called virtual reality (VR). Yet about half of those in both samples and across all groups say they would be somewhat or very interested in experiencing VR. More than half of those surveyed in both countries and across nationals and expat groups said they would be interested in sharing their VR experiences via social media.

Conclusions

Our survey findings demonstrate that in Qatar and the UAE, social media and mobile media are heavily used as a means of both private and public communication. Across time, especially among Qatari nationals, social media use, particularly Twitter, is on the rise. Moreover, the survey evidence obtained suggests that public interest across all segments in both countries is substantial for content designed for mobile. This includes interest in augmented reality and virtual reality.

An important issue is the degree to which AR/VR users want sociability and interaction with others, whether those others are copresent or distant. Also, there is an increasingly important distinction between immersive content vis-à-vis AR and VR experiences. Our findings indicate that, although users have significant interest in sociality while in these media environments or accessing them with distant and/or copresent others, their sociability interests are slightly greater in the VR arena.

Useful in this analysis is a consideration of the special or unique pressures on expatriates versus Qataris or Emiratis living in their homeland. This can also be considered as a question of exigencies of environment versus personal choices and preferences. Put differently, are there unique demands for those who live abroad, or it could be perhaps that those who live abroad are in some way unlike those who decide to stay in Qatar or the UAE? For expatriates, they are not citizens of the country in which they are working and residing. They often are in country temporarily. They may have family in distant lands, and these connections may influence their interests in mobile communication and in particular types of content. This, of course, could affect any generalizations drawn from these data but also aid in interpreting the bigger picture. These factors may affect the convergences and dissimilarities among the usage patterns of both groups. This may also influence rationales as to why those differences may occur.

The question of digital divide may also be a topic of analytical interest. On the one hand, in a data-free assumption, this might not be conceptualized as a public policy problem in terms of media production and access per se. On the other hand, it may indeed be one in terms of potential audience size. To put it differently, it may be the case that language, phrasing, micro content or delivery platforms could be heavily differentiated by socioeconomic groups. If so, certain significant audiences would be omitted from the likelihood/ability of availing themselves of these new media offerings.

Although it may seem obvious to people who pay attention to these issues, a theme worth emphasizing is the way the entire world is going mobile and that mobile connectivity is the wave of the future.

In terms of future directions, it is worth considering questions of social interaction and sharing and missing and perhaps even cocreation. For example, how do people manage personal vs. task-/work-related activities? How do they stay in touch with those they would like to but avoid contact from less desirable sources? These might include hackers, spammers, advertisers and unpopular people. How do they deal with information overload and the increasing pressure to be available from the last thing at night to the first thing in the morning? Considerations of religious practice may also be relevant to mobile media content choices. And, once again, the question of various types of digital divides ranging from entertainment to technology, including the demographic/age component, may be worthwhile to pursue. How much do people depend on and participate in ratings of content? How much producer/consumer and coproduction activity takes place? What is the level of interest across demographic categories in such processes? What effect does this line of activity have on the competitive posture of media companies and on national norms and policies concerning content guidelines?

Note

* With input from Ian Dunham, Rutgers doctoral student and Pavlik's research assistant.

References

Gengler, Justin. (2015). *Group Conflict and Political Mobilization in Bahrain and the Arab Gulf: Rethinking the Rentier State*. Bloomington: Indiana University Press.

IPSOS. (2016). Retrieved 5 January 2018 from https://directory.esomar.org/country179_United-Arab-Emirates/r1515_Ipsos-UAE.php

Mersey, Rachel Davis, Edward C. Malthouse and Bobby J. Calder. (2010). "Engagement with Online Media." *Journal of Media Business Studies* vol. 7, no. 2: 39–56.

Rosenthal, Sara and Kathleen McKeown. (2011). "Age Prediction in Blogs: A Study of Style, Content, and Online Behavior in Pre- and Post-Social Media Generations." HLT '11 *Proceedings of the 49th Annual Meeting of the Association for Computational Linguistics*. Portland, Oregon. Retrieved 21 March 2018 from http://anthology.aclweb.org/P/P11/P11-1077.pdf

Salmon, Charles T. and John Spicer Nichols. (1983). "The Next-Birthday Method of Respondent Selection." *Public Opinion Quarterly* vol. 47: 270–276. Retrieved 5 January 2018 from www.jstor.org/stable/2749026

SESRI [Social and Economic Survey Research Institute]. (2017). Retrieved 5 January 2018 from http://sesri.qu.edu.qa/

Wintour, Patrick. (5 June 2017). "Gulf Plunged into Diplomatic Crisis as Countries Cut Ties with Qatar." *The Guardian.* Retrieved 1 July 2017 from www.theguardian.com/world/2017/jun/05/saudi-arabia-and-bahrain-break-diplomatic-ties-with-qatar-over-terrorism

5   Public engagement

Introduction

Measuring engagement with media has, at best, presented a sticky wicket for researchers and practitioners alike. So, of course, changing the geographic setting to the Arab world and framing the content set around mobile media, including experiential and immersive experiences such as virtual reality and 360-degree videos, only serves to complicate matters a little further. While we have in previous chapters carefully examined the externalities of the region and discussed the role of mobile media innovation and use broadly, the purpose of this chapter is to explore the state of engagement research including that with mobile media content, to present a theoretical framework for our examination, and then to offer our findings from a quasi experiment testing potential interest in specific mobile media content in the Gulf states region.

Contemporary understanding of user engagement

Journalists often think of engagement as a multidimensional variable that comprises time spent with content; interaction with that content, including clicking on embedded links and commenting when such a feature is available; and the related use of social media, whether it be public, such as posting to Twitter, Instagram or Facebook, or private, such as sending a text message to a friend or colleague. Publishers have so much data at their disposal that, in fact, being overwhelmed by statistics – and the uncertainty of what matters – has become an oft discussed issue in the industry. "When everything is measurable and everything is tracked, the problem is no longer a paucity of meaningful data but rather how to separate the signal from the noise," explained Jason Alcorn in a 2017 *MediaShift* article on the potential role for artificial intelligence in data management.

> And in a very real way, analytics are noise. From the real-time analytics screens, often many of them, that hang in newsrooms to alerts in

Slack and via email to multiple analytics tools running in newsrooms for product, ad, revenue and editorial teams, data can be as much a distraction as a tool to help people do their jobs better.

Worse than an overabundance of data is that there is no agreement in the industry or the academy about what engagement is or how to measure it. As media senior editor Lucia Moses noted in Digiday, "Publishers may like to talk about engagement, but there's no industry standard for it" (Moses, 2016). Even among digital measurement services such as ComScore, Parse.ly and Alexa, there are different approaches to measuring the seemingly same thing, including time spent on site (Arendt, 2016). Providers vary, by example, in their abilities to directly measure traffic; in sampling size and quality; and in how engaged a user must be, including whether a browser tab needs to be open or an action, such as clicking or scrolling, needs to occur.

Even without consensus on engagement, there are still provable trends. In our increasingly mobile world, Pew Research Center, using Parse.ly data, has detected distinguishable differences among media. From mobile devices, more referrals to news content come from Facebook as opposed to Twitter (Matsa, 2016). However, average engaged time, which Pew defines as any time that a user spends engaged, such as scrolling, clicking or tapping (Mitchell, Stocking and Matsa, 2016), is longer when content is accessed through Twitter (133 seconds for long-form content accessed through Twitter by comparison to 107 seconds for long-form through Facebook; for short-form content, 58 seconds via Twitter and 51 seconds via Facebook). In apps specifically, Flurry Analytics noted that 2016 saw 365 days of growth (Khalaf, 2017). Usage, defined by opening an app and recording a session, grew by 11%, and time spent in apps grew by 69% as compared to 2015. What was remarkable about 2016 was that it was the first time that some categories of use suffered while others soared. Flurry called 2016 "the year social ate media and telcos," driving home the point that social and messaging apps grew 394% in 2016, as compared to 2015. In the same time period, news and magazine app sessions were 5%, and music, media and entertainment app sessions grew by only 1%. It is a mobile environment that has particularly challenged producers of news. Practically speaking, we see news organizations pivoting to "all-in" strategies to increase engagement and ultimately paid subscriptions (Wilkinson, 2017). The digital magazine *Slate*, by example, launched a *Slate Plus* membership and a number of efforts to increase – and prove – its loyal user base. It has launched a handful of new podcasts, redesigned its daily e-newsletter and increased comment moderation with particular attention to measuring and acting upon the metric of total engaged time. "When we have first time visitors that come to Slate and read two or three articles and spend a minute and a half or two minutes, we want that to be reported and credited in this loyalty initiative," explained Slate's Director of Research Anna Gilbert (Moses, 2016). "And we think that those every-day visitors, or those twice-a-week visitors, are also captured really well. They're worth far more than drive-by visitors who quickly leave the site."

We have also seen the podcast strategy emerge from news producers in the Gulf states. In November 2017, Al Jazeera launched Jetty, a podcast network. The organization positioned Jetty as the forum for developing relationships of some depth that were first established by AJ+, its social news brand with outlets in several countries, which has a demonstrated history of developing breadth. "Compared to what works on Facebook, the dynamics of podcasting and the audio space is almost the reverse," General Manager of Audio at Al Jazeera Kaizar Campwala explained. "In podcasting, acquisition is very expensive, but if you do it right and produce good content, you can have incredible retention numbers. You can really build real loyalty. That's a powerful thing and something we're really interested in understanding and getting good at" (Bilton, 2017). International news providers such as *The Economist* have, in fact, used the expanse of data to create content-based audience growth strategies. *The Economist* "used a ton of data and analytics gleaned from a massive social audience that was more than ten times the size of the paying customers" to determine they were facing a perception gap among nonpaying users: a large portion of them were using *The Economist* content but still saw the brand as primarily serving financial types working to make more money (MinOnline, 2017). In response, *The Economist* started serving robust "topical and provocative" content with an advertising chaser. "The pages are created to showcase the content, maximize data capture and segment our audience for further marketing," SVP Digital Media Mark Beard explained (MinOnline, ibid.). "[Typically] they click on six or more content units before they subscribe" (MinOnline, ibid.). *The Economist* may, in part, be learning from its international brethren. News organizations across Europe, the South Pacific and Latin America are utilizing internal content scoring systems that aggregate data around the economics of content to provide actionable information to editors about the likelihood of an article to trigger much valued subscriptions or to be prosperous on social media.

Social media has received the preponderance of attention in conversations about the broader Middle East primarily due to the political and sociocultural revolutions that marked the turn of the decade. And while the abundant use of social media for political news is reflective of the region, as an Associated Press (AP) study later noted, it is only one means by which people in Egypt, Saudi Arabia and the UAE – where the study focused – interacted with media (Guest, 2015). "Consumers in the Middle East are avid consumers of news, and want to access a broad range of content from a broad range of sources" (Guest, 2015, p. 7). In fact, audiences are just as likely to express a desire to consume political content as technological news, and two-thirds or more of them are interested in entertainment, science, sports, business and finance. What AP notes with regard to engagement is that the MENA audience is significantly more likely than other global consumers to extend their interactions with television broadcasts online. Specifically, about 65% of audience members share content through their social networks at least five times a week, and 59% of consumers who access online news say they discover most of that content through social media channels.

With the power of social interaction, we see the emerging role of new technologies in enhancing these experiences. While broad adoption of virtual reality (VR) may be years away, a study commissioned by Facebook in 2017 pointed to the potentially strong role it could play in engagement (Neurons Inc., 2017). When comparing one-on-one conversations in person to those in virtual reality, where the interaction occurred via an avatar, the study found that VR participants were able to establish authentic relationships that required about the same amount of cognitive efforts as their in-person counterparts. Additionally, "people in the virtual reality group told us they were surprised by how comfortable they felt revealing this personal information in the new environment," according to the report. "Several noted that interacting in virtual reality can reduce appearance-based judgments." As with 360-degree video, virtual reality takes advantage of the first-person viewpoint, which turns out to have empowering characteristics.

The New York Times was among the first news organizations to recognize the value of such technologies in increasing engagement with content. In late 2015, *The Times* delivered a million Google Cardboard VR headset to its subscribers. More than 600,000 downloaded the corresponding NYT VR app, which has since expanded its reach through the Oculus Store for Samsung Gear VR. In addition, each day *The Times* presents 360-degree videos – life on Mars, the Houston Astros World Series parade, floating schools in Bangladesh – in its The Daily 360 series. What is interesting about *The Times*'s approach is that it utilizes both 360-degree cameras and VR for content, recognizing that consumers control their experiences. They call it "immerse yourself, your way." (*The New York Times*, 2018). Use a "smartphone for those just starting out; Google Cardboard for more focused viewing; Daydream View or Samsung Gear VR for the ultimate experience" (*The New York Times*, ibid.)

Because of the growing audience for 360-degree videos and virtual reality, we have also seen the emergence of this crossover technology between 360-degree cameras and virtual reality in cultural organizations. In Peter Leung's *Night Fall*, a VR 360-degree dance film featuring the Dutch National Ballet, you are positioned as a member of the troupe. Similarly, the

English National Ballet produced Giselle VR, a two-minute adaptation of Akram Khan's production, and the Royal Ballet reimagined the snow scene from *The Nutcracker* (Thompson, 2017): "360-degree video technology offers unprecedented access and astounding visuals," explained Candice Thompson in her exploration of the trend (p. 28). "Using an omnidirectional camera or several cameras, every angle is captured and the resulting footage stitched together. During playback online, the viewer has the option of exploring the entire panorama" (p. 27).

And, as Facebook notes in this study, while virtual reality may be currently beyond the scope of the majority of media companies and consumers, 360-degree video has broader market reach, and attention to it as a tool of engagement is well-founded. Both technologies allow for immersive storytelling across platforms with key differences. As mentioned, both VR and 360-degree video are from a first-person viewpoint. However, in a 360-degree video, the consumer is in the position of the camera. VR, alternatively, tracks the motions of the viewer, thereby providing her complete control of her experience. This freedom extends to the storytelling as well. In 360-degree videos, the content creator determines the narrative arc. Consumers may pause or replay, of course, but only in VR does the viewer have total control of the narrative based on her interaction with the content. We are at the beginning of understanding engagement with these new media, and work in this area is best informed by what we have known about engagement with other media.

Historical underpinnings of engagement research

In the academy, scholars have brought a rich tradition of studying engagement and even more potentially relevant variables to bear. This early history began in the study of involvement in the 1980s. The challenge in capturing the first 40 years of this line of research into a theoretical construct is that the definitions of involvement were innumerate and often conflicting. Following a checkered first ten years of involvement research, which was almost exclusively in the field of advertising, Andrews, Durvasula and Akhter (1990) offered in a seminal study of a framework for involvement. At that time, the team called involvement "one of the most controversial topics in advertising research" (Andrews, Durvasula and Akhter, 1990, p. 27). Calling immediate attention to the domain of the individual, Andrews and colleagues stated that "involvement is an individual, internal state of arousal with intensity, direction, and persistence properties" (ibid., p. 28). They then cited its antecedents and its consequences. There were two categories of antecedents: (1) personal needs, goals and characteristics, including cultural values, the degree to which an object has ego relevance and personality factors; and (2) situational and decision factors, including purchase occasion, object usage, degree of decision irrevocability, perceived risk of decision and size of decision consequences. And involvement, according to the research, resulted in three potential consequences: (1) changes to search behavior, including increasing complexity of the decision process, increased time spent and greater perceived product attribute differences; (2) changes to information processing, including increased recall and comprehension and increased cognitive response activity; and (3), most desirably, persuasion or enduring attitude change.

One of the clear values of this early work is that it introduced engagement, nee involvement, as a multidimensional construct. The risk to a full understanding of media engagement, however, is that much of the research that followed remained in the advertising domain, with meaningful consequences. In 2006, the Advertising Research Foundation provided this definition: "Media engagement is turning on a prospect to a brand idea enhanced by surrounding context." This perspective demotes media content – even the best journalism or fact-based content produced by non-news organizations such as museums – to "surrounding context."

Max Kilger and Ellen Romer (2007) cast their engagement research in terms of broad dimensions (inspirational, trustworthy, life enhancing, social involvement, personal time-out, and advertising attention or receptivity) and channel-specific dimensions (television: personal connection, near and dear; Internet: interactivity/community, enjoyment/ attraction; and magazine: image impact). Kilger and Romer were able to connect such dimensions to the likelihood of purchasing products, extending the attention to advertising, valuable but not as comprehensive as the media diets we are considering of consumers in the Gulf states. Recognizing the complexity of the media environment, using data produced by the Media Management Center at Northwestern University (now known as the Media Leadership Center of which one of the authors of this book is the executive director) and the Magazine Publishers Association of America (now the Association of Magazine Media), researchers introduced the concept of experiences. As Ed Malthouse, Bobby Calder and Ajit Tamhane (2007) found, experiences were multidimensional – and collectively could be considered engagement. But the remarkable part of their findings is that the context of the advertising mattered. The way a reader experiences a magazine matters to the effectiveness of the advertising in that magazine. "People who find that the stories in a magazine absorb them also have more positive reactions to the advertising in the magazine," according to the researchers. "Therefore, other things being equal, an advertisement in a magazine with absorbing stories is worth more to the advertiser than the same ad in a magazine that provides lower levels of this experience" (ibid. p. 14).

From this tradition, Malthouse and Calder began with Rachel Davis Mersey, a Northwestern colleague and a coauthor of this book, to develop a predictive model of engagement that further refuted the idea of content as context. Mersey, Malthouse and Calder (2010) defined engagement as "the collective experiences that readers or viewers have with a media brand" (ibid. p. 40). These experiences, informed by the earlier work of Malthouse and Calder, paralleled the dimensions developed by Kilger and Romer (2007). Mersey, Malthouse, and Calder specifically studied eight experiences: (1) social facilitation, (2) temporal, (3) stimulation and inspiration, (4) self-esteem and civic mindedness, (5) intrinsic enjoyment, (6) utilitarian, (7) participation and socializing, and (8) community. What is most important about this research is that relying on both exploratory factor analysis and second-order confirmation factory modeling, they found that these eight experiences actually parse into two types of engagement, personal engagement and social-interactive, confirming engagement as a multidimensional variable that may be influenced by a brand's attention to individuals' experiences with media.

In this model, all media content – advertising, editorial, brand positioning, events – were related experience and therefore engagement. This era of research shed a different light on earlier studies on additional variables relevant to engagement. Todd McCauley and Limor Peer (2014) of the aforementioned Media Management Center, for example, found that, in addition to editorial and advertising content, service elements created positive feelings for newspaper readers 18 to 34 years old. McCauley and Peer found that the cost of home delivery, accuracy of billing, customer service, availability, condition and access could all create "good service" experiences.

With this we clearly understood engagement as a complex construct built on the back of a variety of experiences related to content and noncontent variables. Engagement most certainly was a predictor of advertising effectiveness. However, what remained unclear was the potential of engagement to help us understand individuals' relationships with media products. Then Mersey, Malthouse and Calder (2012) were able to prove in later work that, in fact, reader experiences and engagement, are shown to affect reader behavior even more than satisfaction does. "Media organizations themselves should focus on understanding how to create experiences across multiple platforms including newsprint, websites, tablets, and mobile phones," the authors argued (p. 707). Now the research undertaken for this book expands on the work of Mersey, Malthouse and Calder and that of others and builds on the premise that content type, as previously discussed, is a factor that contributes to audience or user engagement alongside the subject matter or substance of the content or message.

Theoretical model of user engagement with mobile media in the Gulf states

Based on the state of user engagement research previously outlined, we hypothesized that Type IV content – that which is original to the digital environment and also optimized for the qualities or capability unique to digital platforms – will lead to the greatest level of user interest. Notably, as we have seen, digital-first content, produced and disseminated with attention to the media channel and the audience, has seen meaningful results in terms of engagement and ultimately, in some cases, creating paid subscribers. While we recognize an array of definitions of engagement among the industry and scholars, to address this instability, our definition of user engagement used here focuses on levels of interest.

As such, we anticipate the lowest level of respondents' interest in Type I content and a moderate level of interest in Type II and Type III content. The rationale for these predictions is straightforward. When content is designed for the medium on which it is experienced, in this case digital and mobile, the user's interest will be maximized. Further, content customized to the individual, especially in terms of user's preferences, location and context, will heighten user's interest.

Quasi experiment study of mobile media engagement in the Gulf states

Our research follows a tradition of studies examining individuals' interest in emerging media. The most relevant example of such an approach came from the Associated Press that, as we discussed previously in this chapter, examined the potential for video content in the Middle East and North Africa. In it, respondents from Egypt, the Kingdom of Saudi Arabia and the United Arab Emirates answered whether they agreed with "I am more likely to access news stories with a video than just text or sound" and "Watching video news clips improves my understanding of news." While such a methodology relies on respondents' self-awareness, it has proved to be insightful. The Associated Press found, for example, that there is a demand for video news across the region. In the aggregate, 75% of people said they were more likely to access news stories with video content, and 83% said video news clips improves their understanding of the news (Guest, 2015, p. 21). As the report concluded: "The challenge for news providers is clear: how can they get the right video content, at the right quality and embed it into the right online platforms to attract and retain their audiences? In the future, online video should be an integral piece of their digital strategy, not simply a bolted-on extension of their offline content" (ibid., p. 22).

Examination of data from our 2015 Qatar study reveals a general preference for video content, confirming findings of the Associated Press's 2014 study of the region. However, our work offers further points and an attempt to answer the AP's call for what is the "right" content. One, there is ambivalence regarding new media modes such as augmented and virtual reality, a point that we will discuss further. Two, there are differences among subgroups based on interest in the subject matter, education and age. To do so, we relied on a quasi experiment in which we randomly assigned 600 interviewees in Qatar and the United Arab Emirates into six groups of 100. Each respondent was administered the same survey except that each of the six groups was asked an additional question pertaining to one of six alternative forms of mobile content. We placed this question toward the end of the survey after we had already asked questions about augmented reality and virtual reality and before the final general questions. We preceded this unique item with a question asking about respondents' interest in a relevant cultural site. In Qatar, the Museum of Islamic Art designed by I. M. Pei on a peninsula near the dhow (a wooden Qatari boat) harbor. In the UAE, the Burj Khalifa, the world's tallest building with multiple observation decks and a restaurant (in addition to hotels, residences and office space). We briefly examined the effect of interest, discussed shortly, and then used interest as a control variable in analysis of the following question:

Important cultural sites in Qatar/UAE offer various ways for people to experience them using their mobile phones, but not everyone likes to experience these sites in the same way.

(1) For you personally, to what extent would you be interested in reading on your mobile device a brief text description of the Museum of Islamic Art/the Burj Khalifa.

(2) For you personally, to what extent would you be interested in hearing via your mobile device a brief audio, spoken word description of the Museum of Islamic Art/the Burj Khalifa.

(3) For you personally, to what extent would you be interested in seeing on your mobile device a photograph of the Museum of Islamic Art/the Burj Khalifa.

(4) For you personally, to what extent would you be interested in watching via your mobile device a brief video description of the Museum of Islamic Art/the Burj Khalifa.

(5) For you personally, to what extent would you be interested in viewing via your mobile device an augmented reality overlay (a 3D photograph or graphic) of the Museum of Islamic Art/the Burj Khalifa.

(6) For you personally, to what extent would you be interested in experiencing via your mobile device a 360-degree video of the Museum of Islamic Art/the Burj Khalifa.

We repeated the quasi-experiment a second time, asking each respondent a second version of the question, meaning each group of 100 was asked about their interest in a second form of presentation on the content on their mobile device, thereby effectively doubling the sample size. This design allows us to compare potential engagement with different mobile content formats.

First, we found that, as we expected, interest in the subject matter, or what we have called subject salience, was an important intervening variable. When considering subject salience as a dichotomous variable, low-interest individuals were significantly less likely to express a desire to engage with mobile content across all media (text, audio, photo, video, 3D photo and 360-degree video) in Qatar and the UAE. This confirms our initial hypothesis that catering to an individual's preferences – in this case proximity and interest – matters. This finding comes as little surprise to researchers or practitioners. If you are able to find people interested in the subject that you cover with your media product, those individuals are more likely to spend time and become more deeply engaged with your content. But the power of subject salience becomes more evident and more interesting as we examine it as a four-category scalar response for respondent in Qatar, as shown in Figure 5.1.[1]

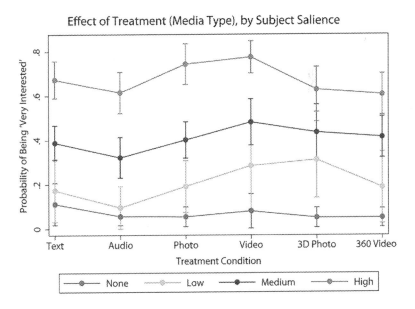

Figure 5.1 Interest in mobile media content type by subject salience in Qatar

As shown, each dot represents the precise predicted values or probability estimates for each category, and the corresponding color-coded bars are the 95% confidence intervals for those estimates. As you see, interest in prose, audio, photo and video through mobile devices follow an expected pattern set forth in the dichotomous evaluation. When considering 3D photos and 360-degree videos, things get more complicated. There is no significant difference among respondents' interest in 3D photo mobile content, except those who have no subject salience. The details are more complicated for 360-degree video. Notably, respondents with high subject salience are significantly more likely than all others to be interested in engaging with 360-degree video content through their mobile devices. Other respondents hang more tightly together. There is no significant difference in interest in 360-degree video content between those with no or little subject salience. Similarly, there is no significant difference between those with moderate or little subject salience. Additionally, as the AP detected in its work in the region, the interest in video content is higher than in any other medium for all groups except those with no subject salience. Further, the interest in 3D photo and 360-degree video on mobile is equal to or greater than interest in audio content.

The narrative among high and moderate subject salience respondents in the UAE is even more distinctive as shown in Figure 5.2, where it is also clear that overall subject salience is significantly lower than that in Qatar.

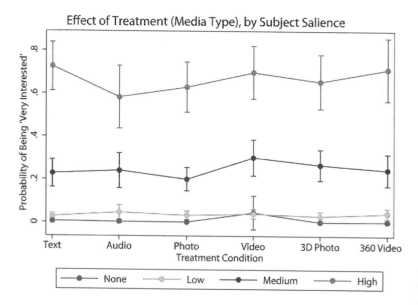

Figure 5.2 Interest in mobile media content type by subject salience in the UAE

We hypothesize that this lower level of subject salience is indicative of the cultural site we selected for study. The data still allow us to examine differences among and between groups.

Those with high subject salience are significantly more likely to have interest in all forms of mobile media content, and their interest level in 3D photo and 360-degree video is equal to or greater than traditional audio and photo content. While those with moderate subject salience are notably lower than we saw in Qatar, uniquely in the UAE, these individuals are significantly more likely than those with little or no subject salience to express interest in all mobile media forms. In addition, for these respondents, video, 3D photo and 360-degree video all rank as more interesting than text, audio and photo. Collectively, the data from Qatar and the UAE suggest that media leaders in the Gulf states should consider the opportunity in emerging mobile media, such as 3D photos and 360-degree videos, as potential audience builders. Content delivered in these forms via mobile devices is less likely than traditional print, audio and visual media to be mediated by subject salience. Additionally, current interest in these emerging media is at least consistent with interest in traditional media across groups, and interest is likely to grow as the media become more commonplace.

Realizing the power of subject salience, to extend our examination, we must control for subject salience. To do so, we utilize a predicted probability generated from an ordered logistic regression because subject salience is a categorical variable. This allows us to account for the idea that, while interest is ordered from low interest to high interest, the distances between the categorical responses are not necessarily equal and to further to reframe the question as how likely a respondent is to be very interested in a mobile content form based on his subject salience. We are able to offer more insight in broader trends, after controlling for subject salience, that could guide media leaders further in determining for which audiences they should develop the next generation of mobile media.

In Qatar, we find no effects for preference in media type after controlling for subject salience based on gender or nationality (Qatari or expatriate). The same holds true in the UAE with regard to gender or nationality (Emirati, Arab expatriate, Asian expatriate). Although it is worth noting that both countries show favor for mobile video content, Qataris express a preference for video content as opposed to all other forms of storytelling. And for them, interest in 3D photos and 360-degree videos is equal to or greater than interest in text, audio and photos. In the UAE, women are more interested in alternative forms of storytelling – video, 3D photo and 360-degree video – than text, audio and photos. Men in the country express the most interest in video, followed by 360-degree video. The stories for education level and age are not as simple. First, consider education level as shown in Figure 5.3.

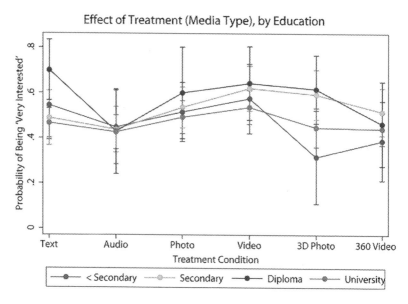

Figure 5.3 Interest in mobile media content type by education level in Qatar, controlling for subject salience

After controlling for subject salience, in Qatar, those with university degrees are significantly less likely than those with high school diplomas or the equivalent to have an interest in mobile written content. In fact, across all categories, with the exception of 3D photo and 360-degree video, the absolute level of interest among university graduates is less than those with less education. A point about which we can only hypothesize might be an effect of subject matter. That is, university graduates in Qatar are potentially more likely to consider themselves already informed about the Islamic Museum of Art and therefore express less interest in related mobile content. What we are able to conclude, however, is that interest in 360-degree videos is fairly consistent with interest in pure audio content among all groups except those with less than a secondary education, representing an area for potential growth. Further, those with a high school diploma or higher are even more interested in 3D photos than in 360-degree photos.

In the UAE, where we have hypothesized the effect of the selection of the Burj Khalifa on lower subject salience, we see further evidence of such in an examination of the relationship between education and interest level in alternative media forms when controlling for subject salience, as shown in Figure 5.4.

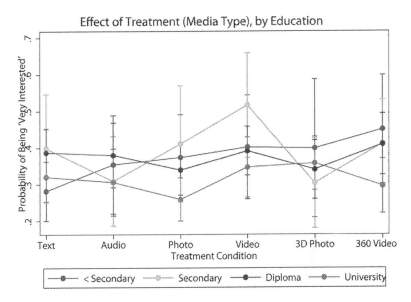

Figure 5.4 Interest in mobile media content type by education level in the UAE, controlling for subject salience

While there are no significant relationships among groups, we see overall interest level in content to fall as education level increases, although it is not a perfect relationship. Among those with less than a secondary education, interest is highest in 360-degree video and lowest in text content, indicating an unsurprising lack of interest in reading and perhaps insight on the value of immersive content for less educated audiences. The story is more consistent for those with a high school diploma or equivalent, but again we see a suggestion that immersive 360-degree video content may have appeal.

Therefore while media producers might presume a class effect of mobile media preference in which higher-class individuals or those with more education would favor more advanced technologies, we have initial evidence that immersive technology such as 3D photos and 360-degree videos could have broader appeal. Where education is more likely to come into play is subject salience. While our work stops short of fully addressing the role of subject matter in interest, we hypothesize that those with more education are seeking material on more complex or advanced topics. This reinforces the need of media producers in the region to deeply understand their target audiences and directs our investigation into one of the fastest growing populations in the Gulf states, young people.

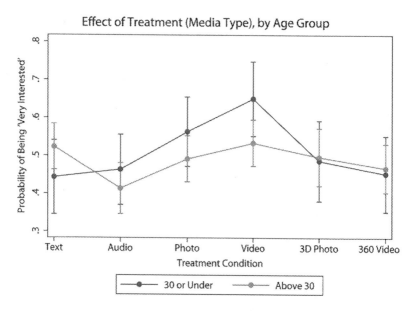

Figure 5.5 Interest in mobile media content type by age in Qatar, controlling for subject salience

The effect of age in the region presents an even murkier picture. Figure 5.5 shows all respondents in Qatar as grouped younger than 30 years old and older than 30 years old, and there is no significant difference in interest in any mobile content type based on age. While there are no significant differences in the UAE either, it is notable that the absolute values suggest that older respondents are more interested in video than in any other medium. This differs from the Qatar data, where younger respondents are more interested in video than in any other medium.

When we examine Qataris separate from expatriates, as shown in Figure 5.6, we see that Qataris younger than 30 years are more inclined, although not significantly so, toward the new technologies of 3D photos and 360-degree video relative to older citizens, but the treatment effects are not stronger than – and if anything are weaker than – that of the basic video treatment.

There is some evidence based on the five-category age plot, shown in Figure 5.8, that the younger-than-25-years-old Qatari group may be more receptive to these new mobile technologies compared to video, but there are not enough data to say this definitively, with the results being only suggestive.

In the UAE, as shown in Figures 5.9 and 5.10, age is more confounding.

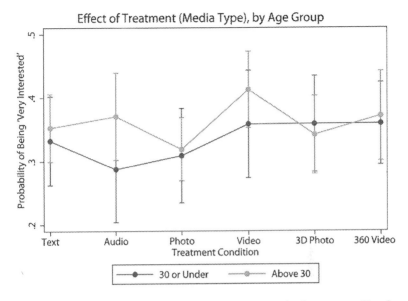

Figure 5.6 Interest in mobile media content type by age in Qatar, controlling for subject salience

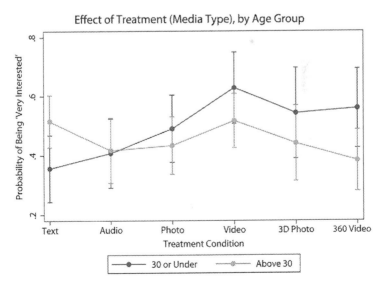

Figure 5.7 Interest in mobile media content type of Qataris only by age (dichotomous), controlling for subject salience

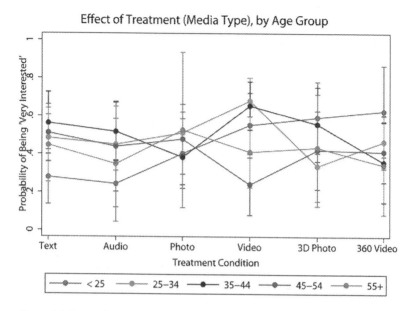

Figure 5.8 Interest in mobile media content type of Qataris only by age (5 categories), controlling for subject salience

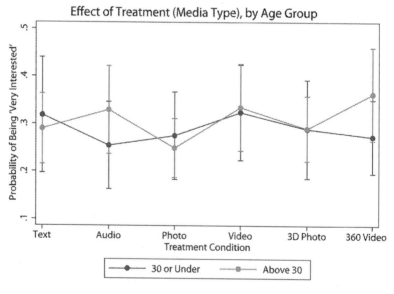

Figure 5.9 Interest in mobile media content type of Emiratis only by age (dichotomous), controlling for subject salience

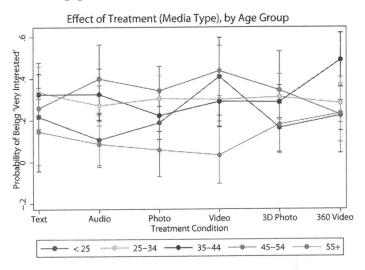

Figure 5.10 Interest in mobile media content type of Emiratis only by age (5 categories), controlling for subject salience

Older Emiratis are most interested in mobile 360-degree video content and younger Emiratis in text content. The five-category age plot suggests that this effect may, in part at least, be due to the interest of Emiratis 35 to 44 years old in 360-degree video; however, the data are not definitive on the effect of age.

The opportunity for mobile media engagement in the Gulf states

While the collective picture across the region is quite complex, the value of an expansive exploration of interest in mobile media content through this quasi experiment is that it allows us to offer guidance to media producers and researchers in the region. First, it is essential to find meaningful connections between potential audiences and content areas covered. Our research confirms the significant effect of subject matter salience. Producing content just because the technological capacity exists is ultimately wasteful and will likely limit the audience's engagement with new forms of mobile storytelling. The real opportunity lives at the intersection of audience interests and technological capacity. Therefore, investment on the part of media producers to understand the needs and interests of their audience would be worthwhile.

Second, media producers should consider opportunities for growth into emerging mobile media. Although there are exceptions, mobile video content has the most consistent appeal in the region, in part confirming our hypothesis that content optimized for the qualities or capability unique to digital platforms will have the highest level of user interest. Where we generally see less interest is in 3D photo and 360-degree video content. While there is a suggestion that the youngest Qataris and 35- to 44-year-old Emiratis are an exception to this trend, findings refute the suggestion that all Type IV content (that which is original to the digital environment and also optimized for the qualities or capability unique to digital platforms) leads to greater interest. A posteriori, we could conclude that these emerging media – 3D photo and 360-degree video – are simply too new to see a significant effect across the Gulf states. Media producers should, however, not concede the opportunity to be market leaders here. Mobile video may serve as a gateway to introduce consumers to emerging mobile content forms of 3D photos and 360-degree videos. We know that the media leadership in the region is poised to tackle the mobile media market, which we will explore more deeply in the next chapter.

Note

1 Four response options: no interest, low interest, medium interest and high interest in the subject matter (in Qatar, the Museum of Islamic Art, and in the UAE, the Burj Khalifa).

References

Alcorn, Jason. (16 October 2017). "Artificial Intelligence Is Coming for Publishers' Analytics." *Mediashift*. Retrieved 5 January 2018 from http://mediashift.org/2017/10/intelligent-analytics-coming-publishing/?utm_source=API+Need+to+Know+newsletter&utm_campaign=f41aae2513-EMAIL_CAMPAIGN_2017_10_27&utm_medium=email&utm_term=0_e3bf78af04-f41aae2513-31691285
Andrews, J. Craig, Srinivas Durvasula and Syed H. Akhter. (1990). "A Framework for Conceptualizing and Measuring the Involvement Construct in Advertising Research." *Journal of Advertising* vol. 19, no. 4: 27. ABI/INFORM Global. Retrieved 5 January 2018 from www.researchgate.net/publication/261591648_A_Framework_for_Conceptualizing_and_Measuring_Involvement_Construct_in_Advertising_Research
Arendt, Kelsey. (29 September 2016). "The Analyst's Corner: How to Benchmark Engaged Time." *Parse.ly*. Retrieved 5 January 2018 from https://blog.parse.ly/post/4490/analysts-corner-benchmark-engaged-time/

ARF (Advertising Research Foundation). (2006). Engagement. Retrieved 5 January 2018 from www.thearf.org/research/engagement.html

Bilton, Ricardo. (1 November 2017). "With Its New Podcast Network, Jetty, Al Jazeera Will Use Facebook Watch to Rope in New Listeners." *Nieman Lab*. Retrieved 5 January 2018 from www.niemanlab.org/2017/11/with-its-new-podcast-network-jetty-al-jazeera-will-use-facebook-watch-to-rope-in-new-listeners/

Guest, Matthew. (2015). "Spring Tide: The New Era for Video News in the Middle East and North Africa." *Associated Press (AP)*, pp. 7, 21, 22. Retrieved 5 January 2018 from www.ap.org/research/video-news-insights/springtide/english.html

Khalaf, Simon. (12 January 2017). "On Their Tenth Anniversary, Mobile Apps Start Eating Their Own." *Flurry Mobile*. Retrieved 5 January 2018 from http://flurrymobile.tumblr.com/post/155761509355/on-their-tenth-anniversary-mobile-apps-start

Kilger, Max and Ellen Romer. (September 2007). "Do Measures of Media Engagement Correlate with Product Purchase Likelihood?" *Journal of Advertising Research*: 313–325.

Malthouse, Edward C., Bobby J. Calder and Ajit Tamhane. (Fall 2007). "The Effect of Media Context Experiences on Advertising Effectiveness." *Journal of Advertising* vol. 36, no. 3: 7–18, 14.

Matsa, Katerina Eva. (9 May 2016). "Facebook, Twitter, Pay Different Roles in Connecting Readers." Pew Research Center. Retrieved 5 January 2018 from www.pewresearch.org/fact-tank/2016/05/09/facebook-twitter-mobile-news/

McCauley, Todd and Limor Peer. (July 2014). Content and Service: Current Drivers of Key Experiences. Evanston, IL: Readership Institute. Retrieved 5 January 2018 from www.yumpu.com/en/document/view/38787129/content-and-service-current-drivers-of-key-experiences

Mersey, Rachel Davis, Edward C. Malthouse and Bobby J. Calder. (2010). "Engagement with Online Media." *Journal of Media Business Studies* vol. 7, no. 2: 39–56, 40.

Mersey, Rachel Davis, Edward C. Malthouse and Bobby J. Calder. (2012). "Focusing on the Reader: Engagement Trumps Satisfaction." *Journalism & Mass Communication Quarterly* vol. 89, no. 4: 695–709, 707.

MinOnline. (25 October 2017). "Legacy Media Puts an Intense New Focus on Audiences." *MinOnline*. Retrieved 5 January 2018 from http://www.foliomag.com/wp-content/uploads/2017/10/min102317.pdf

Mitchell, Amy, Galen Stocking and Katerina Eva Matsa. (5 May 2016). "Long-Form Reading Shows Signs of Life in Our Mobile News World." Pew Research Center. Retrieved 5 January 2018 from www.journalism.org/2016/05/05/long-form-reading-shows-signs-of-life-in-our-mobile-news-world/

Mitchell, Amy, Jeffrey Gottfried, Michael Barthel and Elisa Shearer (7 July 2016). "Pathways to News." Pew Research Center. Retrieved 28 March 2018 from http://www.journalism.org/2016/07/07/pathways-to-news/

Moses, Lucia. (28 September 2016). "How Slate Tried to Wean Itself from Fly-By Facebook Visitors Favor of Loyal Regulars." *Digiday*. Retrieved 5 January 2018 from https://digiday.com/media/slate-increased-loyal-visitors-56-percent/

Neurons Inc. (9 January 2017). *Facebook.* Retrieved 5 January 2018 from www.facebook.com/iq/articles/how-virtual-reality-facilitates-social-connection

The New York Times. (2018). "NYTVR." Retrieved 5 January 2018 from www.nytimes.com/marketing/nytvr/

Thompson, Candice. (17 March 2017). "Is Virtual Reality the Next Big Thing in Audience Engagement." *Dance Magazine*, 27–28. Retrieved 5 January 2017 from www.dancemagazine.com/virtually-part-of-the-ballet-2314184948.html

Wilkinson, Earl J. (22 October 2017). "Scandinavia Emerges as Gold Standard in Digital Subscriptions." *INMA.* Retrieved 5 January 2018 from www.inma.org/blogs/earl/post.cfm/scandinavia-emerges-as-gold-standard-in-digital-subscriptions?utm_source=API+Need+to+Know+newsletter&utm_campaign=b1f2efa8a3-EMAIL_CAMPAIGN_2017_10_25&utm_medium=email&utm_term=0_e3bf78af04-b1f2efa8a3-31691285

6   Media adaptation in the Gulf

Introduction

Network-enabled mobile media technology is fueling disruptive change in the media marketplace. Smartphones and tablets have ushered in a wide range of possibilities for innovation in the realm of digital media content creation, design, distribution and access. Nielsen has reported that three in five, or about 60%, of mobile subscribers in the United States have smartphones. Research in Qatar and the Gulf indicates that mobile penetration is even greater in the Middle East. Some 70% of people use smartphones, and 22% use tablets. Poised for even further change in the mobile arena is a new generation of wearable digital devices, such as head- or wrist-worn, Internet-enabled devices (e.g., Fitbit, a wearable, wrist-worn exercise monitoring device that can measure, among other things, the user's physical activity such as walking and respiratory rate) and smart watches.

Interviews with media industry leadership in Qatar and the Gulf region suggest increasing use of innovation strategies to create and distribute content designed for mobile media. These media have digital, mobile presence, and some organizations are developing content uniquely designed for the mobile platform, including augmented and virtual reality. The development of new strategies for content innovation signals the possibility to heighten public engagement. Building on public traditions of mobility and communication in Qatar and the Gulf region, such innovation in mobile media content, including news, brings the potential to increase public participation (e.g., user-generated content) in news and other forms of media content.

In this chapter, we follow the introduction with a discussion of the findings of in-depth interviews with media leaders in Qatar and the Gulf region with regard to their mobile media content strategies and the role of innovation. In the conclusions, we look at the implications for the theoretical framework outlined earlier in the book with regard to adoption and diffusion of mobile media and content innovation in Qatar, the UAE and the Gulf region.

The blockade of Qatar and the significance of social media

As this study was in the field, a dramatic series of events occurred that more than underscored the role of mobile media, the digital landscape and especially social media where Qatar was at the center of the action. With no warning, on 5 June 2017 four countries, led by Saudi Arabia and including Egypt, Bahrain and the United Arab Republic, broke diplomatic relations with the State of Qatar and imposed a land, sea and air blockade. Saudi Arabia and the UAE surround and make up Qatar's entire land borders while the country, a peninsula, juts out into the Arabian Gulf. This blockade (called a "siege" by some) was allegedly ignited by a hack of Qatar's state-run Qatar News Agency, a few weeks earlier on 24 May. The hack involved the insertion of what Qatar said was a fake news report in which the Emir of Qatar was purported to have made critical and hostile statements about his neighbors, something that was almost immediately denied as the Qataris removed the offending content.

This dustup in the Gulf followed the shorter-term breach of diplomatic relations by the same countries in 2013 and heralded a continuing disagreement among the four Gulf Cooperation Council (GCC) countries and Qatar. Egypt stood with the Saudis as it had its own dispute with Qatar dating to the Arab Spring of 2011 when social media was again at the heart of the revolutions that followed there and elsewhere across the Arab world.

Startled by the severing of ties with critical allies and suppliers of food, building materials and more, the Qataris waited for an explanation, and it came on 23 June when the blockading countries issued a set of demands that included the closure of Al Jazeera, the powerful satellite network based in Qatar and others. The demands and Qatar's reaction drew the interest of major powers and was eventually debated at the United Nations. While there was a continued threat of a hot war with armed conflict that would have seriously breached the security of the region, what ensued was an information war when the blockading nations pushed their demands as they accused Qatar of funding terrorism and terrorist activities, although critics found it curious that the accusers were themselves frequently cited as supporters of state-sponsored terrorism (Katzman, 2017). In Saudi Arabia and the UAE as well as Bahrain, much less in Egypt, local media were filled with accusatory articles and claims about Qatar as an outlier national among the GCC.

Social media were especially vicious, with hostile tweets and other messages supporting the blockade with the UAE going so far as to impose a cyber security restriction that made it unlawful for anyone in their territory to express positive views about Qatar with the threat of a fine and a prison sentence up to 15 years – and this for a positive tweet or other communication. Coverage in Qatar was more restrained, though the country used the blockade to organize a resistance tied to support for the Qatari Royal family and a flurry of wall posters and giant images of the Emir on the sides of the buildings. Accompanied by social media messages, the Qatari response was one of resilience and resistance to the demands and loss of its sovereignty.

Externally, there was massive media coverage, especially in English language media. The story was fed by a renewed American alliance with the Saudis and the powerful Saudi Crown Prince convincing U.S. President Donald Trump that its cause was just and that Qatar was an exporter of terrorism. *The New York Times* reported extensively on the situation and described the situation Qatar finds itself in as "the fight of its life" (Walsh, 2018).

Conversely, an important, data-driven analysis published by the Baker Institute for Public Policy at Rice University casts historical doubt on the efficacy of the blockade (Collins, 2018, p. 1). Collins writes, "Centuries of history reveal a simple strategic truth: embargoes and blockades frequently fail to coerce states into making policy changes sought by the embargoing countries and often create unintended consequences."

In his blockbuster book, *Fire and Fury*, about the first year of the Trump presidency, Michael Wolff (2018) provides some possible insight into what led the president to his position:

> It was, in dramatic ways, a shift in foreign policy attitude and strategy – and its effects were almost immediate. The president, ignoring if not defying foreign policy advice, gave a nod to the Saudis' plan to bully Qatar. Trump's view was that Qatar was providing financial support to terror groups – pay no attention to a similar Saudi history.

Also central to this scenario was the transition to new era of leadership in the Kingdom of Saudi Arabia. Wolff explains, "Enter the Crown Prince of the House of Saud, Mohammed bin Salman bin Abdulaziz Al Saud, age thirty-one. Aka MBS" (p. 231).

Wolff elaborates, noting the digital media engagement of MBS (2018, pp. 224–225):

> The fortuitous circumstance was that the king of Saudi Arabia, MBS's father, was losing it. The consensus in the Saudi royal family about a need to modernize was growing stronger (somewhat). MBS – an inveterate player of video games – was a new sort of personality in the Saudi leadership.

Meanwhile, Qatar's U.S. Ambassador Dana Shell Smith demurred and pointed to a report that suggested any flirtation that Qatar had with so-called terrorist organizations was under control and declining. Secretaries of State and Defense Rex Tillerson and John Mattis opposed the blockade and declared that Qatar was a valued U.S. ally and that it even hosted the largest U.S. military base in the region. On the heels of this support, President Trump, recently back from an Arab summit in Saudi Arabia, sided with the blockading counties in a tweet, thus throwing U.S. foreign policy in disarray. While other major powers also came forward to stem the blockade, the U.S. role was weakened in a region where its power and prestige often holds sway. During this geopolitical crisis, which was discussed at the annual U.N. General Assembly in New York, dueling PR firms and propaganda campaigns ensued. As a study by Northwestern University in Qatar titled "International Coverage of the Qatar during the Blockade" (2018) indicated, Qatar seems in the short run to be winning the PR war with a narrative befitting a tiny, though rich country bullied by its neighbors.

Media leaders, mobile media content strategies and innovation in Qatar and the Gulf

The story of the blockade is complex and nuanced and to some extent goes beyond our concerns here, but suffice it to say that mobile media devices and the content of social media were very much at the heart of the conflict from its very beginning. That information war continues as this is written. The blockade, however, underscores the importance of mobile media, not simply as technological platform but as a powerful weapon in geopolitics and global security. What happened in Qatar is a cautionary tale about how swiftly and lethally social media can have great consequences. And the Gulf, a media-rich nation where digital media has penetrated deeply, may be one of the first tests for mobile media as a stimulus for a geopolitical conflict.

Following is a set of case studies of mobile media content strategies at enterprises operating in Qatar, the UAE and the Gulf region. These cases suggest that mobile media represent a key part of the communication strategy for organizations operating in Qatar and in the Gulf more widely, reflecting an interest in incorporating innovation in the mobile content arena in the region. Innovative approaches to content developed uniquely for mobile platforms especially designed for communities in Qatar and the Gulf region are somewhat more limited and embryonic in development, although some more innovative efforts are underway.

We have generated a roster of more than 100 enterprises engaged in innovative approaches to mobile media content delivery in Qatar and the

Gulf region (QMIF, 2013). These include Al Jazeera Media Network, Doha Film Institute, Doha News, Firefly Media, Google, iLoveQatar.net, Ooredoo, Qatar News, Sport360.com, Thomson Reuters Middle East, and Universal Music Group. We developed a full roster of the leaders of these organizations operating with mobile media in the region.

These case studies offer a profile of the state of mobile media content innovation adoption based on the five categories of adopters of innovations Rogers (2003) identified. Our findings signal confirmation for earlier research, which demonstrates that in general, early adopters of an innovation, called "innovators," constitute a small portion (about 2.5%) of all potential adopters of an innovation. These innovators are likely to become advocates for the innovation. They facilitate category two, the early adopters. They represent a slightly larger portion of the total (about 13.5%). Category three includes early majority adopters. They comprise about one-third of the total (34%). Category four includes late majority adopters. They comprise about one-third (34%). Category five includes the laggards or late adopters, a relatively small group (about 16%). We are beginning to assess the extent to which this pattern prevails in Qatar and the Gulf region with regard to organizations utilizing mobile media.

Methods overview

In cooperation with partner Deloitte, in 2016 we conducted interviews with 100 individuals in positions of leadership at organizations identified in the Year 1–phase one operating with mobile media for communication in Qatar and the wider Gulf region. These interviews focused on each organization's adoption of mobile media innovations and strategies for producing content for mobile media in Qatar and the Gulf region.

Interviews were conducted face-to-face in English and generally were 20–30 minutes in duration. Organizations included a mix of private and government entities. The general parameters included individuals in the following positions of leadership:

1   Media HR manager: 80% private; 20% government
2   Media manager: 80% private; 20% government
3   Strategic communications manager: 70% private; 30% government

Mobile media content strategy questions

Each interviewee was asked the following four questions regarding their mobile media content innovation strategies for Qatar and the Gulf region. These questions are designed to provide a foundation for understanding the extent to which these organizations are developing innovative strategies for mobile content and as a test of Rodgers's innovation model.

1   To what extent do you utilize mobile media in communicating with your audiences in Qatar and the Gulf region? If not at all, why not?
2   What is the general strategy you employ with mobile media in reaching those audiences?
3   In what ways do you design the content for the mobile media platforms you employ?
4   In what ways, if any, do you see content designed for mobile media as an advantage in effectively communicating with your audiences in Qatar and the Gulf region?

Ten media leaders were interviewed in Year 1. Data have been maintained in anonymous and confidential form, in adherence with IRB guidelines. By country they include Qatar: 5, UAE: 3, Lebanon: 2.

A foundation for case studies in mobile media content innovation in Qatar and the Gulf region

Following is a summary of the findings that provide an initial basis for the case studies that will be fully developed over the course of this three-year research project.

To the first question, "To what extent do you utilize mobile media?" responses include the following strategies:

*   "Everything today is on mobile" (Managing director, Qatar).
*   "I don't think about it as a separate thing, mobile is part of the strategy" (Author, Lebanon).
*   "All of our marketing efforts for our products are through digital marketing and mobile, we have apps for most of our products" (Market intelligence manager, UAE).
*   "For every product we have to look at a mobile product or app that users will want" (Market intelligence manager, UAE).
*   "It has become the first strategic platform we are building on" (Managing director, Qatar). Social media is seen as an essential mobile media tool.
*   "Social media is extremely important here and the content we produce has to be viewed on smartphone platforms" (Managing director, Qatar).
*   "There is more prevalence of platforms like Snapchat in Qatar" (Managing director, Qatar).
*   "What I don't want to find is that we are doing things with external interests that are not being communicated through social media" (Head

of corporate affairs, Qatar). The size of the mobile media audience has increased drastically in the past few years, though desktop still has a presence.

- "Smartphone penetration in Qatar is among the highest in world" (Head of corporate affairs, Qatar).
- "50% of the Qatari population is below 20 years old, a big part of our audience will come from mobile channels" (Head of corporate affairs, Qatar).
- "Our type of viewers are [sic] getting notifications and quickly having a look at the website."

As these responses indicate, mobile media have become a central part of the communication strategy for organizations operating in Qatar and the Gulf region. The results also indicate that the extent to which organizations have developed content uniquely formatted for mobile is at varying stages of development, from content optimized for social media such as Snapchat to a spectrum of smartphone platforms. Moreover, the strategies rest on an understanding of the unique qualities of the public in Qatar and the Gulf region and the importance of designing content for that public.

To the second question, "What is the general strategy you employ?" responses include the following but in general indicate that they are applied typically on a case-by-case basis.

- "Our strategy depends on the brief" (Managing director, Qatar). It should be noted that a brief refers to a business brief, which is a document designed to help promote goods and services to customers and clients, or expand profits, or provide solutions to industry problems.
- "Our strategy depends on the client" (Managing director, Qatar)
- "Our strategy depends on the product" (Author, Lebanon). However, many companies also define general guidelines.
- "There is a high level strategy in our company" (Product owner, UAE).
- "We have clear guidelines in Instagram" (Head of corporate affairs, Qatar).
- "Our strategy is to be active, engaging, authentic and professional" (Head of corporate affairs, Qatar).
- "My target for the team is to be the most engaged international energy company in Qatar" (Head of corporate affairs, Qatar).

As these responses indicate, a substantial number of organizations have developed strategies specifically for mobile media content, including guidelines that emphasize audience engagement and activity, as well as content authenticity. Yet these strategies are still relatively embryonic in utilization of the novel capabilities of networked mobile platforms such as immersive content (e.g., virtual reality) and geolocated content (e.g., augmented reality).

To the third question, "In what ways do you design the content?" responses include the following, but in general indicate that mobile media strategies are focused on a high level of customer, user or public engagement or interaction.

- "The important thing is how to communicate interactively, not only give information but create engagement" (Managing director, Qatar).
- "Strong UX: when we are designing for mobile we are very conscious about how people use mobile" (Author, Lebanon).
- "When you are communicating through the mobile channel, typography and user experience are very important" (Author, Lebanon).
- "We have recently made our websites more mobile friendly" (Editor, UAE). Mobile media content is generated in-house or outsourced to external teams.
- "We have a digital team in house" (Managing director, Qatar).
- "We have a team of 100 people in Beirut which does a lot of content gathering and not necessarily content generation. A lot of new content created is outsourced" (Market intelligence manager, UAE).
- "Both technicians and designers work together to set up the functionality which is set according to the project guidelines" (General manager, Qatar). Format and content design are critical features of mobile media platforms in the region.
- "The more creative, the better" (Managing director, Qatar).
- "Some images require resizing but until now we don't change content. Moving forward may require changing some of the content but haven't done that yet" (Editor, UAE).
- "Our approach is inspired on what we used to do for the web" (General manager, Qatar).
- "Content doesn't matter much in this part of the world. We expect something to be beautiful and then fill it up with content" (General manager, Qatar).

As these findings suggest, although some organizations have developed advanced mobile content strategies, some are still in the early stages of adoption. One respondent indicates images represent an area for innovation, but this organization has yet to adapt its images for mobile.

To the fourth question, "In what ways do you see content as an advantage?" responses include the following, but in general indicate that the mobile platform is considered more accessible for target audiences.

- "Most clients are keen to see how they can evolve their brands through their mobile media" (Managing director, Qatar).

- "When the product has an open wide audience then mobile makes sense" (Market intelligence manager, UAE).
- "Mobile channel is much more intimate than desktop" (Author, Lebanon).
- "It's a very important channel right now – more than a generic channel because you can reach people very easily and at any time" (Senior art director, Lebanon). Mobile channel is more flexible and dynamic than desktop communications.
- "On the desktop you have longer time to adapt and innovate; mobile is more competitive" (Author, Lebanon).
- "We give more importance to design in mobile as it is a much faster channel, with very quick interaction with customers. You have to grab their attention to stop them and make them look at the ads" (Senior art director, Lebanon).
- "You need to be very reactive, things change quickly, especially with the platforms (e.g., Facebook)" (Author, Lebanon).

As these results suggest, most organizations recognize the significant advantages of that content optimized for mobile. These advantages include both the unique design capabilities of mobile media as well as the potential to interact with target audiences. The results also suggest that media management lines of activity are heavily populated with leaders in innovation. Our interviews revealed that there is a heavy concentration of Rogers's Type I and II actors. Although this conclusion may not be surprising because activities in this arena, namely mobile media creation and consumption, are perhaps the most fast moving and rapidly changing of any realm of human activity, they are important from a decision-making perspective. In this light, Rogers's schematic can be an important analytical tool in making judgments about personnel management and programs that stimulate innovation.

Following are lessons that emerge from an analysis of current mobile media innovation in Qatar and the Gulf region.

1   Present brands through their mobile media.
2   Employ mobile as a much more intimate channel than desktop.
3   Mobile channels are more flexible, dynamic and competitive than desktop communications.
4   Design in mobile as it is a much faster channel, with very quick interaction with customers, capturing their attention more effectively.
5   Mobile allows rapid reaction and response in communication content, especially with the social media platforms (e.g., Facebook)

Following are media operating in Qatar and the Gulf region that our research identifies as having developed unique mobile media.

1 Al Jazeera Media Network
2 Doha Film Institute
3 Doha News
4 Firefly Media Server
5 Google
6 iLoveQatar.net
7 Ooredoo
8 Qatar News
9 Sport360.com
10 Thomson Reuters Middle East
11 Universal Music Group
12 OSN

These 12 companies represent a breadth of media industries operating in Qatar and the Gulf, including journalism, entertainment, and music. News-related enterprises include the Al Jazeera Media Network, Doha News, Thomson Reuters Middle East and Qatar News. Founded in 1996, the Al Jazeera Media Network is Doha based and operates as a multinational news organization.

Illustrative of Al Jazeera's mobile media content innovation strategy is the development of Contrast VR (Contrastvr.com). "Contrast VR is Al Jazeera's new immersive media studio" (Al Jazeera Media Network, 2017). It offers original immersive media experiences on a range of stories designed especially for mobile media platforms. Contrast VR coproduces and distributes a growing amount of VR and 360 video content in immersive format meant to enable audiences to access stories in-depth via wearables and handheld platforms, as well as via laptop or desktop displays. Productions include "Contrast VR Originals," featuring high-end documentaries about pressing regional and global issues. Examples of available productions include "I Am Rohingya," "Oil in our Creeks," and "Forced to Flee." "I am Rohingya," for example, offers users a cinematic VR experience produced by Contrast VR and AJ+. It was recorded in 360 video format on location in Kutupalong Refugee Camp in Cox's Bazar, Bangladesh.

Doha News is a Qatar-based independent online news organization founded in 2009. Thomson Reuters Middle East (2017) is the regional operation of the global news service Thomson Reuters founded in 1799 (2008). Qatar News is a regional news agency founded in 1975 (2017).

Doha Film Institute is a cultural organization founded in 2010 by Sheikha Al-Mayassa bint Hamad bin Khalifa Al-Thani. Its mission is "dedicated to film financing, production, education and the Film Festivals."

ILoveQatar.net is a news and information site focused on the cultural life of Qatar (2017).

Firefly Media is a Qatar-based media agency (2017).

Ooredoo is a Qatar-based international telecommunications company (2017).

Sport360.com (2017) is an international media enterprise delivering coverage of sport, including sport in Qatar and the Gulf.

OSN is a Dubai-based international media entertainment company delivering video entertainment via satellite and online in Qatar, the Gulf and the Middle East (2017).

Universal Music Group is an American-French global music company operating in Qatar and the Gulf (2017).

Google is a U.S.-based "multinational technology company specializing in Internet-related services and products." (2017). Founded in 1998, Google operates in Qatar and around the world.

Relevant to the development of mobile content strategies as well may be certain psychological and sociological dimensions that media managers address. This could be both on the level of content production and consumption. Hence, it may be a competitive dimension or even an advantage to consider problems of multitasking and information overload. Is there a competitive advantage to having a system designed with these factors in mind? These are topics for future research.

References

Al Jazeera. (2017). "Careers." *Al Jazeera Media Network*. Retrieved 5 January 2018 from http://careers.aljazeera.net/en/about/about-us.html

Al Jazeera Media Network. (2017). "Contrast VR." *AJAM*. Retrieved 3 January 2018 from http://contrastvr.com

Collins, Gabriel. (22 January 2018). "Anti-Qatar Embargo Grinds toward Strategic Failure." *Baker Institute for Public Policy, Rice University*. Retrieved 23 January 2018 from www.bakerinstitute.org/media/files/files/7299ac91/bi-brief-012218-ces-qatarembargo.pdf

Dennis, Everette E. (17 January 2018). "International Coverage of the Qatar during the Blockade." A Crisis Report. Northwestern University in Qatar.

Doha Film Institute. (2010). *DFI*. Retrieved 5 January 2018 from www.dohafilminstitute.com/

Doha News. (2009). *DohaNews.co*. Retrieved 5 January 2018 from https://dohanews.co/

Firefly-Me. (2017). *Firefly-me*. Retrieved 5 January 2018 from www.firefly-me.com/

Google. (2017). "About." *Google*. Retrieved 5 January 2018 from www.google.com/intl/en/about/

ILoveQatar. (2017). *ILoveQatar*. Retrieved 5 January 2018 from ILoveQatar.net

Katzman, Kenneth. (27 December 2017). "Qatar: Governance, Security, and U.S. Policy." *Congressional Research Service*. Retrieved 19 January 2018 from https://fas.org/sgp/crs/mideast/R44533.pdf

Ooredoo Qatar. (2017). *Ooredoo Qatar*. Retrieved 5 January 2018 from www.ooredoo.qa/portal/OoredooQatar/home

OSN. (2017). *OSN*. Retrieved 5 January 2018 from www.osn.com/en-sa/home

Qatar News Agency (QNA). (2017). "Qatar News." *QNA*. Retrieved 5 January 2018 from www.qna.org.qa/en-us/News/QatarNews

QMIF (Qatar Media Industries Forum). (2013). "Qatar News." *Northwestern University in Qatar*. Retrieved 5 January 2018 from http://www.qatar.northwestern.edu/news/events/media-industries-forum/index.html

Rogers, Everett M. (2003). *Diffusion of Innovations*, 5th ed. New York: Free Press.

Sport360. (2017). *Sport360.com*. Retrieved 5 January 2018 from http://sport360.com/

Thomson Reuters. (2017). "Mean." *Thomson Reuters*. Retrieved 5 January 2018 from http://mena.thomsonreuters.com/en.html

Universal Music. (2017). *Universal Music*. Retrieved 5 January 2018 from www.universalmusic.com/

Walsh, Declan. (22 January 2018). "Tiny, Wealthy Qatar Goes Its Own Way, and Pays for It." *The New York Times*. Retrieved 23 January 2018 from www.nytimes.com/2018/01/22/world/middleeast/qatar-saudi-emir-boycott.html

Wolff, Michael. (2018). *Fire and Fury: Inside the Trump White House*. New York: Henry Holt and Company.

7 Concluding reflections
Trends in the next generation of journalism and media

Introduction

The findings of this investigation suggest directions for the development of evolving mobile media content and entrepreneurship in Qatar, the Gulf region and beyond. In this chapter, we examine the implications of this research for the likely next generation of mobile media content, including journalism and other forms in information, entertainment and strategic communications. We examine the advent of wearable media and the potential for media content innovation and public engagement in a wearable media environment in Qatar and beyond.

Following an introduction, we provide a discussion of the implications of the current research for mobile content innovation, as well as preparation of the next generation of journalists and media professionals in Qatar and the Gulf. We offer a reimagining of news and media content for a mobile and social media platform.

Reimagining the news and media content as mobile

In Qatar, the Gulf region and beyond, the emergence of mobile media as a dominant platform for public engagement offers media leadership in journalism and beyond an opportunity for innovation. This opportunity is apparent on at least four levels.

First, media leadership in journalism and other arenas can develop more extensive original content designed for mobile, handheld platforms. The public, both Qatari nationals and expats and others in the Gulf region, have a demonstrated interest in such content. Some innovative media organizations have begun to develop such content, and the public is responding with increased engagement. Further original content optimized for mobile and wearable platforms may greatly increase this engagement, especially if linked to social networking media.

Second, the emergence of immersive and interactive mobile content formats, especially 360 video and augmented reality on handhelds, offers journalists and media leaders the potential to develop content featuring these qualities. The public has demonstrated a clear and growing appetite for such mobile content. As new generations of mobile devices diffuse throughout the marketplace, offering improved capacity to access such content, opportunities for media organizations to design and deliver innovative content will grow, and public engagement is likely to increase in kind. Wearable technology platforms signal further opportunities in this regard, and we explore these shortly.

Third, opportunities to engage the public in interactive communications using social media networks are clear. The public is already widely sharing user-generated content (UGC) via social networks. Evidence we have presented indicates that the public across all sectors, both nationals and expatriates, have a strong interest in sharing new media content forms designed for mobile, including augmented reality and virtual reality.

Finally, designing mobile content that can innovatively and effectively utilize geolocation is another opportunity. Whether through interactive maps, geo-tagged photos and video, and other mobile forms, geolocation is an emergent feature available on mobile platforms. Other interactive and mobile capabilities such as games seem to have less resonance among nationals than among expatriates.

Implications of wearable media for journalism

The development of wearable communications and data technologies as a form of mobile media presents potentially powerful opportunities to engage the public. Evidence we have presented in this book suggests an increasing public interest in content designed for wearable media platforms. As wearable platforms diffuse in Qatar and the Arabian Gulf, including head-worn displays, opportunities to create interactive immersive content will grow. Survey data presented in this book indicate that the public has a significant and growing appetite for such innovative, immersive content. Original, rather than repurposed immersive content is especially likely to engage the public, as the data reported in this book suggest.

In particular, we have offered and tested a model of innovative mobile media content as represented in Figure 3.4. Based on this model, we suggest that media content providers emphasize the design and production of what we call "Type IV" content. It is original, mobile and user optimized with five dimensions or qualities:

1 Responsive design that is fluid and highlights the ease of user experience
2 Interactive, many-to-many, or social networking, with strong support for UGC

3   Intelligent, dynamic and adaptable, location-aware content enabled by algorithms designed to augment human media professionals, including journalists
4   Convergent sight, sound, haptic, and 3D content formats optimized for mobile and wearable platforms
5   Functional content (e.g., supports user action or agency, such as participating or making a purchase), with heightened user control and actionable content

Based on this data foundation, our research suggests at least three possibilities for innovation in journalism and media leadership in Qatar. First, head-worn platforms such as those developed for augmented reality (AR) and virtual reality (VR) are of growing interest in Qatar and the Gulf. Journalists and other media content developers can design immersive, multisensory and interactive content in news reporting as well as in other forms of information and entertainment.

Second, consumers have begun to embrace a variety of other wearable devices such as fitness tracking technology. Such platforms can enable journalism and other media organizations to design content built in customized fashion for each user, such as content that is adapted to their location, patterns of mobility and situation (e.g., health circumstance). Encouraging user-generated immersive content represents a related opportunity to increase public engagement in this arena. Tools for capturing 360 video and creating augmented reality are falling rapidly in price and growing in availability in the consumer marketplace. As these consumer-friendly tools grow in adoption and diffusion, much as drones have done during the past five years, the volume quality of UGC immersive content is likely to develop. Embracing immersive UGC will help to heighten the engagement between media and the public in Qatar and the Arabian Gulf generally.

Finally, journalism and other media enterprises in Qatar and the Gulf can engage users via wearable technologies to share personalized information with family or friends. Sharing unique, immersive experiences represents a novel media format that, while new, is generating increasing public demand. As more sharing occurs, the demand for additional such immersive content is likely to grow in snowball fashion.

Yet it will be critical to maintain a high level of privacy protection and security. Our research indicates that privacy is a paramount concern in Qatar and the Gulf. Moreover, concern about privacy and security is growing, with nationals and expatriates alike expressing concern about how to protect their privacy and security in an age of corporate or government surveillance, as well as threats by online hackers launching cyber attacks from around the globe.

Mobile media and the transformation of the media landscape in Qatar and the Gulf region

Many traditional media companies have struggled to adapt to the changing digital, networked and increasingly mobile media landscape. Around the world, hundreds of newspapers and other print news media have gone out of business, and many tens of thousands of journalists have been laid off. This book has presented findings that media enterprises in Qatar and the Gulf region can employ in adapting to the changing media landscape and in developing innovative content strategies designed for mobile media platforms. The extent to which these strategies succeed may depend on the potential to engage a public that has widely adopted the use of mobile media for their own communications and media experience. While the findings discussed are based on a multi-method investigation in Qatar and the UAE, the evidence suggests that the theoretical implications extend far beyond the region and the profession.

The following discussion examines the implications of advances in mobile and wearable media for the ongoing transformation of journalism and media content in Qatar, the Gulf region and the world beyond.

Based on the evidence presented, we suggest five broad implications for the transformation of mobile content in Qatar and the Gulf and potentially beyond this region. Drawing on the adoption and diffusion model of Rogers and others, these implications are based on a synthesis of three sets of data we have generated in the first two years of the research project in Qatar and the UAE. First, a small set of media leaders are highly engaged in introducing uniquely designed content for mobile media platforms. These early adopters are consistent with the findings of previous research on the adoption and diffusion model. In this study, they are developing content intended for mobile media distribution, access and interaction (e.g., sharing via social media). While some of this content is original to mobile platforms, much is adapted from other media environments. In-depth interviews with regional media leaders suggest that the five-stage model of adoption and diffusion to mobile content innovation pertains in Qatar and the Gulf region. Specifically, our findings confirm the relevance to decisions regarding implementing mobile content innovations of (1) the perceived relative advantage of mobile media content innovation, (2) compatibility, (3) complexity or simplicity, (4) trialability and (5) observability.

Second, the gradual emergence of wearable media technologies presents an opportunity for innovation in Qatar and beyond. As the public increasingly utilizes wearable platforms, and as the public appetite revealed in our surveys will likely continue to grow, content designed and optimized for wearable platforms will present an opportunity to uniquely engage the public. The general research literature suggests that immersive media forms, such as AR and VR, not only are highly engaging but also can help build empathy or understanding of other perspectives. This is consistent with the findings of our research

Third, the public across various subgroups is highly engaged with mobile media. They are heavy users of content delivered to mobile platforms. They are very likely to share such content. Important differences between subgroups should be accounted for in communication strategies. These include differences between Qatari nationals and expatriate communities. Similar patterns of differences exist in the UAE.

Fourth, the foundation of media is continuing to shift and to shift rapidly. Mobile and social media usage is strong and on the ascent. Awareness of types of content designed for mobile and social media platforms is growing across all public segments and in both Qatar and the UAE.

Moreover, the leadership of media and the public are adapting rapidly to this shift toward increasing public engagement in mobile and social media platforms. Journalism and media enterprises have an opportunity to adapt to this changing environment and in many cases are already doing so in innovative fashion, such as Al Jazeera's development of an immersive storytelling initiative designed for mobile and wearable media, including virtual reality. However, the window for adaptation may not stay open long before competing new enterprises step in to fill the public demand for innovative, mobile content demand.

Finally, important contextual considerations should frame any adaptation to the mobile, wearable environment. While geolocation, customization, and immersion are unique content formats, the public and media leadership alike have deep and profound concerns about privacy. Accounting for strong privacy protections will be key to any successful utilization of mobile, wearable media and content designed for those platforms.

In addition, it is essential to consider these changes in the context of the broader geopolitics of Qatar and the Gulf region. As discussed in Chapter 6, the blockade will likely shape the development of mobile media device usage and content, especially as a means of public engagement via social media.

The blockade, however, underscores, the importance of mobile media not simply as technological platform but as a powerful weapon in geopolitics and global security. What happened in Qatar demonstrates how swift and lethal social media, particularly fueled by ubiquitous mobile media, can have great consequences.

Future research will prove vital in continuing to test these conclusions and to help place them in a wider context regionally and beyond. Although we have focused on Qatar and the UAE, the dynamics of the region feature a variety of unique characteristics, and it will be of great value to examine the extent to which the findings presented here with regard to mobile content innovation pertain over time and within a more global context.

Index

360 video 29, 50, 55, 61, 64–65, 70–74, 91, 96
7Days app 55, 57

adoption and diffusion 10, 16–17, 24–27, 35–38, 41, 64, 82, 86, 96
Advertising Research Foundation 66
AJ+ 63
Alcorn, Jason 61
Al Jazeera Media Network 26, 30–31, 40, 55, 63, 83, 86, 91, 98
Arabian Gulf 2, 83, 95–96
Associated Press 63–64, 68–69, 71
Association of Magazine Media 66
augmented reality 23, 26–29, 35–36, 47–49, 55, 58, 89, 95–96

Beard, Mark 63
Boczkowski, Pablo 17
Bower, J.L. 12, 17
Burj Khalifa 69

Calder, Bobby J. 39, 66–67
Campwala, Kaizar 63
Carey, John 17
Christensen, Clayton M. 10, 12–15, 17
content (media) 1–2, 6–8, 11, 15–20, 24–38, 61–80, 87–96
Contrast VR 91

The Daily 360 64
Daydream View 64
Digiday 62
Doha Film Institute 86, 91
Doha News 48, 86, 91
Dubizzle 55, 57
Dutch National Ballet 64

The Economist 63
The Edge 26, 42
Egypt 63–64, 68
embargo (economic blockade) 4–5, 40, 44, 51, 83–85, 98
engagement (consumer, public) 1–2, 8, 24, 26, 35–39, 43, 51, 61–69, 78, 84, 94–98
English National Ballet 65

Facebook 64–65
Fidler, Roger 16
Field theory 12
Flurry Analytics 62
Fromherz, Allen 3–4

Geolocated, Geolocation 26, 36, 39, 89, 95, 98
Gilbert, Anna 62–63
Giselle VR 64
Google Cardboard 50, 55, 64; VR headset 64
Grogin, Gerard 17
Gulf Times 31, 42, 48

Hjorth, Larissa 17
HTC Vive 50

ILoveQatar 26, 30–31, 42, 48, 86, 91–92
innovation ii, 2, 6–8, 10–13, 17–20, 23–28, 31, 35–39, 82, 85–91, 94
Internet 1–2, 4, 11, 23, 31, 35, 46–47, 53–57, 82, 92

Jetty 63
journalism 1–2, 4, 6–8, 13, 17, 35, 91, 94–98

Katz, James 7, 19, 33
Khaleej Times 55, 57
Khan, Akram 65
Kilger, Max 66–67

Leung, Peter 64
Levinson, Paul 19

Magazine Publishers Association of
    America 66
Majlis 2
Malthouse, Edward C. 39, 66–67
Matsa, Katerina Eva 62
McCauley, Todd 67
McKeown, Kathleen 39
Media Leadership Center 66
Media Management Center 66–67
MediaShift 61
Mersey, Rachel Davis 1, 39, 67
methodology 68
mobile media 1–2, 5–8, 15, 23–32,
    35–59, 79, 85–88, 94; apps 26,
    31, 35, 42, 47, 54, 57, 62, 87;
    smartphone 1, 10, 15, 19, 23, 31–32,
    46, 53, 56, 82, 87–88; tablet 23,
    30–32, 46, 53–54, 82
Moses, Lucia 62–63
Museum of Islamic Art 69
Mzad 48

Namshi 48, 55, 57
The New York Times 64
Night Fall 64
Northwestern University 66; in Qatar
    16, 23, 30, 85
The Nutcracker 65

Oculus Rift 23, 50, 55
OSN 42, 48, 91–92

Peer, Limor 67
Pei, I.M. 69
Pew Research Center 62
podcasting 63
Pokémon Go 49, 55
privacy 26, 47, 54, 96, 98

Qatar 1–8, 10, 24–26, 30–31, 35–41,
    46–51, 69–77, 79, 82–92, 94
QatarLiving 48

Qatar National Research Fund
    (QNRF) 1, 8, 35
Qatar University 39
quasi-experiment 70

Rogers, Everett 24–26, 36, 86, 90, 97
Romer, Ellen 66–67
Royal Ballet 65

Said, Edward 5
sampling (sample) 39–41, 44, 51, 62
Samsung Gear VR 64
Saudi Arabia 63–64, 68
Schoenbach, Klaus 16
Scolari, C.A. 15
SESRI 39, 51
Slate 62–63
social (networking) media 4–8, 16,
    24, 29, 31, 38–39, 47, 54–58, 63,
    83–87, 94–95; Facebook 31, 38–39,
    48, 55, 57, 61–65, 90; Flickr 48,
    55; Google+ 31, 38–39, 48, 55;
    Instagram 31, 38–39, 47, 54, 57,
    61, 88; LinkedIn 48, 55; Reddit 48,
    55; Snapchat 47, 54–55, 87–88;
    Tumblr 48, 55; Twitter 31, 38–40,
    47, 55, 57–58, 61–62; Youtube
    38–39, 47, 55
survey research 8, 16, 23, 31, 35, 38,
    40–41, 43, 50–58, 97

Tamhane, Ajit 66
Thompson, Candice 65
Thorson, Esther 16
Type I content 68
Type II content 68
Type III content 68
Type IV content 68, 79

United Arab Emirates (UAE) 1–2, 4,
    10, 25, 35, 51, 63–64, 68–79

virtual reality 24, 27, 30, 33, 35, 50, 55,
    58, 61, 64–65, 82, 95–96, 98
VR *versus* 360-degree video,
    distinctions between 65

wearable media 30, 94; Headworn
    display, platform 96
World Internet Report 16

Printed in the United States
by Baker & Taylor Publisher Services